THE
Country Seasons
COOKBOOK

THE
Country Seasons
COOKBOOK

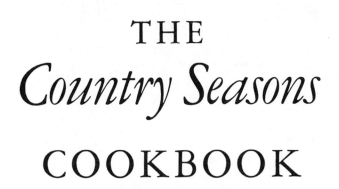

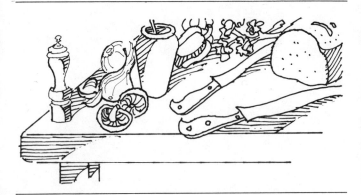

BY GLADYS MANYAN

Drawings by Doug Anderson

Crown Publishers, Inc.　　　New York

To the loving memory of

LOUISA A. NALBANDIAN

a superb cook, a wise mother, and
a woman who brightened every life she touched

Inquiries should be addressed to Crown Publishers, Inc.,
419 Park Avenue South, New York, N.Y. 10016.
Library of Congress Catalog Card Number: 74–80292
Printed in the United States of America
Published simultaneously in Canada by General Publishing Company Lim-
ited.

Designed by George Hornby and Margaret C. Lewis

Contents

Preface

OOKING, I discovered, was not a magic gift suddenly acquired by marriage.

Two vivid recollections of my complete ignorance of the culinary arts concern the time my husband George flushed two soft-boiled eggs down the toilet and I buried my first pies under the zinnias.

Marriage was furthest from my thoughts when I met George. I had other plans. I was pursuing a career in the performing arts—singing.

I had returned to Providence, Rhode Island, after beating the pavements of New York City for several months the year vaudeville died and show business was gasping for breath. The country was in the throes of the worst depression in history, and I ended up broke and back home.

At that crucial period in my life when the future looked darkest, George came on the scene. I fell in love and got married. Poor George! We both discovered that my education in home economics had been extremely neglected, but I was determined to be a successful homemaker. After working at it for thirty-five years, I have made considerable progress. My most significant discovery, perhaps, was the knowledge that cooking is a creative art contributing to good health if wisely practiced.

George was in the laundry business, and I helped out by soliciting new customers as we gradually pulled ourselves out of the depression during World War II. We had a business telephone at home and I also took general calls, acting as a one-man office while George hit the road.

One spring when our sons, Babe (christened George) and Dave, were five and seven years old, George suggested that the three of us take a vacation in the country. He said he would arrange for someone to answer our phone. After investigating the cost of such a vacation and the cost of farms in New Hampshire, I held out for a farm. I argued that the initial cost was only slightly more than the price of a vacation, and we would gain a place to retire in our old age.

George gave in, and one weekend, dressed like hayseeds, we all piled into our panel laundry truck and headed for the New Hampshire hills. We checked out several farms and selected our present home, mostly because it was the only farm with electricity we saw at that time.

Another attraction was the price—$2,300 for twenty-one acres, house, barn, and other buildings. "Other buildings" were two large former chicken coops, a shed between the house and barn, and one in back of the barn. Both sheds collapsed the next winter from the weight of the snow.

The second summer when we took our vacation, we foolishly went overboard on country living—got chickens, a lamb, two pigs, and planted a large garden. Not knowing how to become disentangled, we stayed.

Our daughter Gail joined the family during a February blizzard when Babe was eleven and Dave, thirteen. We ran out of wood for our heating system, a chunk stove, and the farmer who promised to replenish our supply informed us that the blizzard had dropped too much snow, preventing him from getting more logs out of the woods.

While the boys and George were at school and work, I broke up some extra furniture to feed the stove and keep the baby warm. During the remainder of the winter, we scavenged, the boys dragging in old tree trunks and breaking up an old wooden floor left across the road when a house was moved.

We did our share of pioneering before we learned to adjust and to cope with severe winters, fewer modern conveniences, and a much smaller income. I discovered that a garden full of fresh vegetables cut down food costs considerably, but creative cooking was necessary to make vegetables in season appealing when the same ones had to be served so often. In the beginning, too, my knowledge of gardening was so limited I thought planting in hills meant erecting the little hills first; so my cucumber plants seemed to erupt from small volcanoes in our first garden.

I became a health nut gradually—after we switched to organic gardening to eliminate weeding. Other advantages of organic gardening soon were evident. Mulching between rows with hay and leaves prevented the soil from drying out during droughts. Our growing vegetables stayed healthy while those in conventional gardens dried out if not watered. And I became aware of a gradual decrease of harmful insects. Also, worms increased in the soil, and I added more from our worm pit of hybrids. My venture into hybrid worms was one of many projects to supplement our limited family income.

At about the same time, an increase of physicians' bills we could not afford prompted me to think in terms of preventive measures to stay healthy. In between my varied projects, I took time to study nutrition and foods seriously and eventually turned into a dedicated health-food fan. Now, however, I consider myself simply a concerned and sensible cook and homemaker, in this day of present ecological awareness.

This is not a complete cookbook but a collection of our favorite recipes from my venture into creative cooking with wholesome ingredients. It is based on my weekly column in the *Concord* (N.H.) *Monitor*, where I am employed as the Franklin Area bureau chief. I was prompted to write the book to satisfy requests for back columns and recipes and to make available back recipes that some readers missed.

Although I gave up my job when I married, I took a part-time job in the office of the Franklin bureau when Gail was a senior in high school, later becoming chief. Soon after, I started writing a food column that gradually expanded to include my experiences with George in organic gardening. With the proliferation of chemical additives in food and other pollution, I found myself in the Don Quixote role of doing my bit to help influence homemakers, through the column, to buck the unhealthy trend and use pure foods as much as possible. So this is a combination of my love for creative cooking, clean country living, and hope for the healthy future of mankind.

I would like to thank all the readers of my column in the *Concord* (N.H.) *Monitor,* most especially those who helpfully kitchen-tested so many of my recipes and took the time to let me know they had become family favorites. Thanks are also due the numerous non-cooks, including many men, who expressed their enjoyment of the column; to Cris Camarra; and to the *Monitor,* its publisher George W. Wilson, and its editor, and assistant publisher, Thomas W. Gerber, for permission to use some of the material from my columns.

January

A RECENT conversation with Babe, who was visiting us with Judy, our daughter-in-law, started us reminiscing about our first moving trip here after we bought the farm. On a cold blustery January day, we felt warmer just talking about that trip.

In spite of the fact that we lived in a city, our house, owned by my mother, had a huge yard in the rear where we had built a small chicken coop for eight laying hens, which furnished us fresh eggs.

During the morning of moving day, with the temperature already 84 degrees, we packed the hens in a crate, loaded our panel truck with odd-and-end furniture donations, added two cats someone had abandoned the day before in front of our house, made room for our two sons in back of the front seat, and took off with my mother. This was before the day of the turnpikes and, for some reason, we did not try planning a route to bypass Boston.

After the trial of getting through the Boston traffic, we decided to find a cool woody spot to eat our picnic lunch, since we had been on the road for about three hours. The cats were scrambling around in the back and the hens were panting, with their beaks open. George pulled the truck off the road near a grassy glen and we spilled out, each of the boys taking a cat with him. We decided to air the hens, too, so George took out the slatted crate. In spite of the intense heat, we all began to feel better after lunch and cold milk from a gallon thermos.

Babe, who was six then and always the more observant of our two boys, had finished eating first and strayed over to the hen crate. "Mom, there's something wrong with one of the chickens!" he called. George and I dashed over. Sure enough—one of the hens in the crowded crate was acting peculiar. George took her out of the crate and set her on the ground. For a minute we thought she was going to keel over and die. Instead, she squatted and laid an egg—then took off, wings flapping, across the grass.

We all chased after her, the boys heading her off. Gradually we closed the circle, Babe grabbed her by a leg, and George returned her to the crate. Then we repacked the truck, got in and finished our trip, arriving at the farm seven hours after leaving Providence. Now, with the turnpikes, we make the trip in two and one-half hours, but even before the turnpikes we learned to cut our time down to five hours bypassing Boston.

January is a fitting month to bake pastries and quick breads. The weather limits other activities, yet baking will afford a creative outlet for the homemaker and eating pleasure for her family. Hearty breakfasts of pancakes and muffins are in order during this cold month, too.

My quickest pancakes and pastries are made with a basic nutritious mix, which has gone through healthy transitions. This mix will make a fine base for creative baking if it is substituted for the flour in other recipes and you also omit the salt and baking powder or soda in the other recipes. I use the mix exclusively for pancakes and waffles. For waffles or lighter cakes and pastries, I separate the eggs and fold in the stiffly beaten egg whites last thing before baking.

BASIC NUTRITIOUS MIX

6½ cups unbleached white flour	1 cup powdered milk
1½ cups soya powder	⅓ cup baking powder
4 teaspoons salt	2 cups raw wheat germ

Shake all the ingredients in a large plastic bag or canister. Refrigerate or freeze the extra amount that is not needed immediately. I sometimes replace ½ the flour, or all of it, with stone-ground whole wheat flour. The sea salt or pickling salt I use has no additives, so it is saltier. Increase other salt if necessary.

To make speedy pancakes with this mix, beat 1 or 2 eggs with 1 or 2 tablespoons corn oil. Add ⅓ to ⅔ cup milk and enough of the mix for the desired consistency.

OATMEAL PANCAKES

This easy, light, and tasty pancake is another one of our favorites. Do try it.

1 cup quick rolled oats	2 tablespoons corn oil
1 cup hot water or milk	2 teaspoons baking powder
2 eggs, separated	1 teaspoon salt
½ cup cold milk	½ cup flour

Soak the oats in hot water or hot milk about five minutes. Beat the egg yolks with the cold milk and oil. Add to the oatmeal mixture. Combine baking powder, salt, and flour and stir into the oatmeal mixture. Fold in stiffly beaten egg whites. For thinner pancakes, add more milk or another egg.

I sometimes substitute ¼ cup each soya powder and cornmeal for the flour, and stir in in ¼ cup powdered milk if I use water to soak the oatmeal. Either white or whole wheat flour can be used.

BUTTERMILK WHOLE WHEAT WAFFLES

Here is another goody:

2 eggs separated	1½ teaspoons baking powder
2 tablespoons corn oil	½ teaspoon salt
2 cups buttermilk	2¼ cups whole wheat flour
½ teaspoon baking soda	

Beat the egg yolks with the oil and add the buttermilk. Combine the dry ingredients, then add the buttermilk mixture. Fold in stiffly beaten egg whites. The same amount of yogurt, thinned with a little water, can be used instead of buttermilk. For crisper waffles, reduce the flour to two cups.

Whether the winter turns out to be mild or severe, we have found it wise to be prepared for the worst. By January, we are finally ready for anything that may happen. Gradually, from past experience, we have overcome most of the winter catastrophes but one—hazardous driving—which still plagues me, and I become more chicken every year.

Winter driving in snow causes no problems unless I get caught in a blizzard or find myself on the road when the snow is drifting, but driving on ice is something else. Since I have had a few scary experiences sliding off the road, I try to take more precautions every winter.

"It's all in your head," George grunted as he put on my fourth studded snow tire. In case anyone gets the wrong impression, let me explain that one would have to try hard even to feel the worn studs by rubbing a hand over the tires. For one thing, after George put on the stud tires we ordered last year, I found that studs were inserted in only a few of the holes. I was told it was too late to put in more studs since I had driven on the tires and the holes were full of dirt. In spite of what George says, it isn't all in my head.

One icy morning a few years ago when I was driving to work in our pickup with snow treads, the truck took off by itself on the top of a hill. Fortunately for me, the snowbanks on both sides of the road were high. The truck spun around into one bank, catapulted across the road into the opposite bank, hit with enough force to send it back again, turning and twisting during its progress down the hill, and finally stopping against a tree banked with snow.

I was petrified throughout, but kept a death grip on the steering wheel and my foot off the brake. The ride had a slight similarity to the Dodg'em rides we enjoyed in amusement parks as children, only I didn't have any fun on this one. Babe was getting married the next week, and all I could think of was what a terrible time for me to crack up. It finally dawned on me, as I sat in the truck catching my breath, that I was in one piece and unhurt. I carefully stepped out on the slick ice and inspected the pickup. Outside of a bent left bumper where it had hit, nothing seemed amiss. Later, when George got the truck to a garage, he found the battery hanging from one wire.

Another time, when we were paying tuition for Gail to attend junior high school in Franklin, I had to meet the school bus at one point daily and drive her the rest of the way home. While I was parked, waiting for the bus, a sudden heavy snowstorm struck, covering the road and its patches of ice with a white blanket in just a few minutes. We had to go up a long hill on the way home and, partway up, our old sedan shot off the road and into a snowbank. The two of us got out of the car, checked our position, and decided there was no way we could get that auto out. A neighbor with a four-wheel-drive vehicle happened by at that moment and gave us a ride home.

Later, when George got home from work, I told him what had happened.

"How in heck can anyone slide off a road going uphill?" he asked in his usual stentorian tone.

"It was easy!" I replied, staring him down. He let the matter drop and took off with one of the boys, who happened to be at home, to dig out the car.

Although using lard is against my general health rules, I make an exception for pie dough. I think lard is the only shortening for a superior, tender, flaky piecrust, but I buy a brand with no preservatives and immediately make enough dough to use up a one-pound package. I prefer to bake in quantity and freeze the extra amount to use for a quick dessert when needed. Pies should be heated through again to bring out the flaky texture. This pie dough recipe makes six pies or a pan of fruit squares and four small pies.

PIE DOUGH

6½ cups unbleached flour	1 pound lard
1½ teaspoons salt	cold water

You can substitute ¼ cup soya powder and ¾ cup wheat germ for one cup of the flour. Wheat germ enhances the flavor and texture of the crust. Sometimes I also substitute 2 cups stone-ground whole wheat flour for the same amount of white flour.

Stir the dry ingredients with a fork to blend. Work the lard in with a pastry blender or the hands, to the consistency of very course meal. Add enough cold water so that dough will hold together when lifted with a fork. Do not handle the dough more than necessary. If time permits, refrigerate the dough for about 30 minutes.

Make as many pies as desired, and freeze the remainder of the dough. For apple pie, perk up the flavor of flat apples with lemon juice when adding the sugar. Instead of lemon juice, I sometimes add a few pieces of frozen rhubarb. If fruit squares are planned, buy economically priced bulk pitted dates and strung figs sold by the pound.

FRUIT FILLING

1 pound figs and dates mixed	⅔ cup sugar or honey
1½ cups seedless raisins	juice of ½ lemon
4 cups water	1 rounded tablespoon cornstarch

Put the figs and dates through a food chopper. Add raisins, water, sugar or honey, and lemon juice, and boil together for 15 minutes. Dissolve the cornstarch in a little water and add, stirring constantly; boil 1 minute more. Cool.

Use a 12 x 15 inch baking pan for the squares. Line it with a sheet of dough, spread on the cooled filling, and cover with another sheet of dough after moistening the edges of the bottom crust. Seal the edges by pressing with a fork dipped in flour. Prick the entire top with the fork and brush with evaporated milk for a glossy surface. Bake at least 45 minutes in a 400° oven, 30 minutes on the bottom shelf and 15 minutes on the top shelf, until the crust is golden. Cool on a trivet before cutting in squares.

I bake pies in the same manner, leaving them in the oven 45 to 60 minutes. Pies so baked will not have soggy bottom crusts. Since I use glass pie plates, I check the bottom crust before switching a pie to the top shelf or removing it from the oven. Cooling pies on trivets will also help keep the bottom crust flaky.

Most homemakers are familiar with the usual pie fillings, but here are two that are unique and very tasty.

HONEY-RHUBARB PIE FILLING

4 cups rhubarb, cut in pieces	¼ teaspoon salt
6 tablespoons flour	2 teaspoons grated lemon rind
1 tablespoon wheat germ	2 tablespoons oil
(optional)	1½ cups honey

Combine rhubarb, flour, wheat germ, salt, rind, and oil. Stir in the honey. If honey is not available, try sugar.

MOCK CHERRY PIE FILLING

1 cup hot water	1 cup sugar
1 cup raisins	2 tablespoons flour
2 cups cranberries	1 teaspoon vanilla

Combine water, raisins, and cranberries and cook until the cranberries make a popping sound. Stir the sugar and flour together and add to the cooking mixture, stirring constantly and cooking 1 minute more. Remove from heat and add vanilla. Pour in an unbaked shell and make a lattice top.

When we first came to New Hampshire we felt, being city folks, that we were more sophisticated and knowledgeable than our country cousins. We were in for a rude awakening. We got taken so many times I began to wonder if the natives passed the word around to bait the hook when dealing with us.

After we paid for a well that wasn't dug, a chimney that wasn't repaired, and an auto that wouldn't run, we decided to see an attorney. We were waiting in his office, reviewing the circumstances, when it occurred to me that the lawyer, whom a neighbor had recommended, was bound to question our intelligence.

I beat him to the punch. "We're not really stupid, just trusting," I said. "We thought all country folks were honest and trustworthy."

We paid for the well in advance because the man who started digging it said he needed money to buy food for his children. We learned much later, after we hired someone else to finish the job, that he had a drinking problem and we had helped it along.

I take no credit for the auto caper. George was responsible for paying for that hunk of junk in advance. We found out later why the former owner delivered it at night—with the help of friends, he had it pushed into our driveway and quietly left. We never did get that car to run. Eventually, the former owner towed it off our property and we got most of our money back.

We fell for another hard-luck story in the case of the chimney. The chimney sweep also failed to return to complete his job, although he had promised he would. Eventually, we discovered that people were the same everywhere—some good, some bad, some foxy, and some foxier. We're a little less naïve now, though we're both congenital chumps.

Looking back at the hectic days when the children were young and unexpected guests would sometimes arrive for meals, I recall that I often stretched out the food by quickly whipping up a batch of muffins. This easy addition always impressed our guests and enhanced my reputation as a good cook.

I consider muffins the tops in the quick bread category. They can be made in endless varieties with fresh and dried fruits, berries, nuts, and spices. By trial and error I discovered that the trick to making light muffins was to *fold*, not stir, the liquid mixture into the dry ingredients.

Bake all muffins at 400° for 20 to 25 minutes after filling oiled muffin-tin cups two-thirds full. Most of the following muffin recipes make one dozen large muffins.

In all these recipes with the exception of the high nutrition muffins, I sometimes substitute ¼ cup wheat germ for the same amount of flour, or use part stone-ground whole wheat flour. I also add ¼ cup powdered milk to the dry ingredients for extra nutrition, and substitute honey for all or part of the sugar.

Since I consider cooking a creative art, I'm not a stickler for exact measurements. A few grains more or less of baking powder or baking soda do not change the results in baking recipes, so I don't take the time to level off measuring spoons or cups with a knife.

BASIC MUFFINS

2 cups unbleached flour	1 beaten egg
½ teaspoon salt	1 cup milk
4 teaspoons baking powder	4 tablespoons corn oil
4 tablespoons sugar or honey	

Combine the dry ingredients by stirring with a fork. Beat the other ingredients together. Fold the milk mixture into the dry ingredients to blend. Before folding in the milk mixture, add 1 cup blueberries or ½ cup raisins to the dry ingredients for variation.

HIGH NUTRITION BASIC MUFFINS

1½ cups unbleached flour	½ teaspoon salt
4 tablespoons soya powder	2 eggs, separated
4 tablespoons wheat germ	1 cup milk
4 tablespoons powdered milk	2 tablespoons corn oil
4 teaspoons baking powder	4 tablespoons honey

Stir the dry ingredients with a fork to combine. Beat together the egg yolks, milk, oil, and honey, and fold into the dry ingredients. Fold in the stiffly beaten egg whites. For blueberry muffins, add 1 to 1½ cups berries.

BRAN MUFFINS

1 cup whole bran	1 cup unbleached flour
1 cup milk	2½ teaspoons baking powder
1 egg, beaten	½ teaspoon baking soda
4 tablespoons unsulfured molasses	½ teaspoon salt
4 tablespoons corn oil	½ cup raisins

Combine the first 5 ingredients in a bowl. Cover and set aside for about 2 hours (or overnight, for morning breakfast). Stir the other ingredients together with a fork. Fold the bran mixture into the dry ingredients.

OATMEAL MUFFINS

2 cups quick oats	1 egg, beaten
1½ cups sour milk, buttermilk, or plain yogurt thinned with water	½ cup unsulfured molasses
	1 cup unbleached flour
	1½ teaspoons baking soda

Soak the meal in sour milk for about 2 hours. Mix in the molasses and egg. Combine flour and soda, and fold into the meal mixture.

CORN MUFFINS

1 cup unbleached flour	½ teaspoon salt
1 cup cornmeal	2 eggs
4 tablespoons sugar or honey	⅔ cup milk
4 teaspoons baking powder	4 tablespoons corn oil

Combine the dry ingredients by stirring with a fork. Beat together the remaining ingredients and fold into dry ingredients.

DOUGHNUT MUFFINS

1 cup unbleached flour	½ teaspoon cinnamon
½ cup whole wheat flour	½ teaspoon nutmeg
2 teaspoons baking powder	1 egg, beaten
½ cup sugar or honey	⅔ cup milk
½ teaspoon salt	4 tablespoons corn oil

Combine the dry ingredients, stirring with a fork. Combine the other ingredients, and fold into the dry ingredients.

My doughnuts have gone through only one transition because I seldom make doughnuts now. The last time I made them was at a New Year's open house when Gail was home from college and had told friends to drop in. We planned to serve snacks to the few people we expected to come. When her friends arrived bringing their friends, I thought fast and decided to make doughnuts, since I couldn't move out of the kitchen anyway—the house was so jammed.

I made a huge batch, and several youths took turns cutting and frying under my direction. They still talk about what a fun party it turned out to be, claiming the doughnuts played a leading part in its success.

Here is my original recipe.

DOUGHNUTS

2 large eggs	½ teaspoon salt
1 cup sugar	2 tablespoons baking powder
2 tablespoons corn oil	½ teaspoon each nutmeg and
1 cup milk	cinnamon
4 to 4½ cups unbleached flour	

Combine the eggs and sugar in a large bowl. Stir in the oil and milk. Sift other ingredients directly into the egg mixture and stir. The dough should be soft, but if it is too soft the doughnuts will absorb oil when fried. A little experimenting may be necessary to get the right consistency, since the size of the eggs affects the amount of liquid needed. I mix doughnuts by hand without using the electric beater.

Roll out part of the dough. After cutting, combine the scraps with fresh dough to keep the doughnuts that are cut last as light as those cut first. The final scraps can be rolled into a couple of crullers.

Later, I improved on the nutrition in doughnuts by adding ¼ cup powdered milk to the dry ingredients and substituting two cups stone-ground whole wheat flour for the same amount of white flour. Next time I shall add a heaping tablespoon of soya powder to the dry ingredients, too.

Use an extra-generous amount of flour when rolling out doughnuts to prevent their sticking. It can be brushed off before frying them. I have an awful habit of blowing off the excess flour as I place each doughnut into the hot oil. I fry everything in corn oil. (When deep frying, I add a 100-unit vitamin E capsule to the oil because I read somewhere that, otherwise, vegetable oil will oxidize after it has been .

heated once, giving it a rancid odor and flavor.) Drain the doughnuts on paper towels. This makes about 3 dozen doughnuts.

Everyone should be able to make perfect doughnuts with this recipe, tender and delicious. The improved version is by far the better, in my opinion.

PERFECT RAISED DOUGHNUTS

2 packages dry yeast	¼ cup corn oil
½ cup warm water	2 eggs, beaten
4 tablespoons sugar or honey	4 cups unbleached flour
¾ cup warm milk	¾ teaspoon nutmeg or mace
1 teaspoon salt	½ teaspoon cinnamon

Dissolve the yeast in warm water, adding a little of the sugar or honey to activate it. Let set about 5 minutes. Then add the remaining sugar or honey, milk, salt, oil, and beaten eggs. Stir in the flour and spices.

Here, again, I substitute 2 cups stone-ground whole wheat flour for ½ the white flour, and add 4 tablespoons powdered milk to the dry ingredients before combining all the ingredients.

Cover the dough and let rise until double in bulk, about 1 hour. Punch down and knead for about a minute; cover and let stand about 15 minutes while preparing the frying pan, oil, and the paper towels on which to drain the doughnuts.

Cut out the doughnuts and let them set about 30 minutes to rise again. Drop them in hot oil, raised side down, to raise the other side (now on top) while the underside cooks.

For jelly doughnuts: Cut with a biscuit cutter, let rise, and fry. After frying, make a deep slit in the side of each and fill with jelly. I use homemade raspberry jam.

I decided one day to try a batter similar to cream puff dough to make a quick fried snack. The result was yummy—feather-light golden balls, which we dunked in maple syrup and homemade cherry-raspberry-strawberry jam. I am beginning to wonder how I can coordinate a reducing diet with my interest in cooking and eating . . .

GOLDEN BALLS

1 cup water
¼ teaspoon salt
3 tablespoons corn oil

1 cup unbleached flour
4 eggs

Combine water, salt, and oil in a saucepan and bring to a boil. Add flour and stir rapidly for a few seconds. Mixture will form into a compact mass. Remove from heat, cool slightly, and add the eggs one at a time, beating after each one. If convenient, chill the dough for maximum lightness.

Drop dough by teaspoonful into hot oil and fry until golden. Puffs will invert by themselves. I used stone-ground whole wheat flour.

February

U P IN THIS neck of the woods, February is the month that tries men's souls. Our first winter here, in 1947, was one of the worst in history. I don't remember how the rest of my family reacted, but I never expected to survive. To my surprise, we all did, and learned our first lesson in self-reliance.

We had set up two oil space heaters, but soon learned why the neighboring farmers used chunk-wood stoves to keep warm during the bitter cold days. We also figured out why they circled the bases of their homes with ugly tarpaper and why they took a dim view of indoor plumbing.

After our water pipes froze, we bundled up more heavily and returned to the privy, commonly known as the two-holer, at the end of the woodshed. We were thankful we had not destroyed it.

I said we bundled up *more* heavily because I spent the whole winter bundled up. I wore heavy woolen socks and felt boots in the house during the day and removed the boots when I got into bed. We used so many quilts for covering in our icy bedrooms (we closed them off to reserve the little heat from the oil stoves for the two rooms we were living in) that we arose punchy from the weight.

Most of the daylight hours I spent hallucinating on whether it was worse to be cold or hungry. I had never been that hungry, but—in exchange for warmth—was willing to risk it.

As a general rule, the roads were plowed and kept open, but that winter we got snowed in for three days. Babe and Dave, who usually rode their bicycles when possible or walked to the school bus stop, had to snowshoe across the fields. The one precaution we had taken was to buy bearpaws, a type of small snowshoe, for the boys and regular snowshoes for us. We learned to use them.

Since those days, we have come a long way. We insulated and tightened up the house, doing most of the work ourselves, and eventually had an efficient central heating system installed. Finally we could get through the winters comfortably warm and without frozen water pipes. The first such winter came as a pleasant shock.

I still hit bottom with winter doldrums in February, but less often now since Babe, who lives fairly close, in Rehoboth, Massachusetts (Dave and his family live in Florida), built me a lovely glassed-in porch. It has a separate heating unit and thermal-pane glass, which transmits the solar heat when the sun shines.

The completely glassed southwestern end is ideal for a greenhouse. I found a perfect contraption to use for plants, which fits exactly in the area. Made of heavy galvanized metal, this weird gizmo has four boxlike compartments, each the size of a bushel box but deeper. We lined the compartments with stones and filled them with a special composition of soil, which we mixed in an old galvanized tub. I was told the tub—it came with the farm—had been used for Saturday night baths in front of the kitchen stove. Our soil mixture consists of two parts of good, wormy garden dirt (we threw some of the worms back) with one part each of sand and peat moss.

The first year, I planted cherry tomatoes in two compartments, one climbing cucumber plant, which I started in a peat pot, in another section, and herbs in the last one. We realized the potential of the porch too late to start this project soon enough, so had questionable success. Although I hand-pollinated the cucumber flowers with a small paint brush and strung the vine on a tall stake, the winter harvest consisted of three cucumbers, one normal and two warped in shape but edible. The tomato plants were more prolific and bore enough bite-size tomatoes for our winter salads. These plants I pollinated by shaking the branches periodically.

I had potted a pepper plant from the garden and brought it in, but was forced to send it out to freeze in January because it was covered with aphids. Although I tried every safe way I knew to destroy them, they hung on tenaciously. One day when Babe and Judy came to visit, Babe noticed that the window in back of the plant was covered with a new winged variety of aphid. Or perhaps it was some other tiny winged insect, drawn to the aphids. Anyway, that was the death knell of the pepper plant. Babe gingerly carried it out and wedged it in the snow by the kitchen window. It was such a beautiful plant. I mourned as I watched it freeze, collapse, and die.

Now, the indoor winter garden is not a haphazard last-minute venture. I give the plants an earlier start. Fresh, organically grown vegetables in winter are a rare luxury.

During this month, I really enjoy creative baking with yeast dough. I recommend it highly as perfect therapy to chase away the blues and cure frustrations as winter drags on. Use a lump of yeast dough as your basic clay; hang loose and give your imagination free rein. The odor of baking breads and seeing your counters laden with exotic breads and pastries will lift your spirits and give you a sense of creativity equal to that of any artist. And think how you will bask in your family's praise!

Through different phases of my increasing concern with proper nutrition, I have developed three basic doughs that I use for most of my yeast breads and pastries. I have always used unbleached white flour as the least harmful of the white flours.

At first, I began substituting some honey for sugar and corn oil for other shortening, especially after the cholesterol scare. Later, I added wheat germ, soy bean or soya powder, and powdered milk to the flour for greater nutrition. Then I started substituting stone-ground whole-grain wheat flour for part of the flour and, in some instances, substituted the whole-grain wheat flour for all the white flour. Finally, editorials and newspaper articles on the lack of nutrition in white bread and flour scared me into baking most of my breads with stone-ground whole-grain flour.

Many concerned young couples, trying to fight pollution and live wholesome lives, have formed food cooperatives through which they can get stone-ground whole-grain flours at reasonable prices. Some have bought or rigged up grinders to grind wheat and other grains themselves, since the wheat berries will stay fresh for long periods without refrigeration.

I get most of my wheat flour through a friend who buys it wholesale to bake nutritious bread that is sold through natural food stores.

Brown rice and other small grain flours I grind myself in an old, manually operated coffee grinder I bought for twenty-five cents at a rummage sale.

Just to scare you into thinking in terms of good nutrition: Many of the commercial "whole" wheat breads look darker only because of the caramel coloring that is added. Also, there is a difference in whole wheat flours, depending on the method of milling. Only the stone mills pulverize the whole grain, including the wheat germ, in its nutritious state. Modern steel roller mills heat the germ by the rapid friction, reducing the quality and making it susceptible to rancidity. The wheat germ was originally screened out by modern high-speed roller mills because the heated wheat germ gummed up the rollers.

According to the *Mystery of the Mill* by Vrest Orton of the Vermont Country Store in Weston: "This epoch-making discovery allowed the millers to expedite their operations but, more significant, they discovered soon enough that flour from which the live and perishable wheat germ was screened out would keep indefinitely on store shelves."

For further proof of how "dead" white flour is, John Lear in a *Saturday Review* article says most of the vitamin A, 77 percent of vitamin B-1, 80 percent of vitamin B-2, 81 percent of vitamin B-3, 72 percent of vitamin B-6, most of the vitamin D, and 86 percent of vitamin E are removed from the wheat berry during the processing of white flour. A large percentage of the minerals are also removed, he claims, and the balance of one changed in a manner that jeopardizes human health. For further reading on this subject, I suggest *The Chemical Feast* (the Nader's Raiders' book by James S. Turner) and *Consumer Beware!* by Beatrice Trum Hunter.

Faced with these facts, it seems to me our only defense is to find a source of stone-ground whole-grain flour and bake bread and other pastries with it at home.

My baking career began with this:

BASIC YEAST DOUGH

2 packages dry yeast	2 eggs
1 cup warm water	¼ cup sugar
2 cups scalded milk	4 teaspoons salt
½ cup butter	9 to 10 cups unsifted flour

Using a 2-cup measure, stir about 1 tablespoon of the sugar into the warm water and add the yeast. Leave in a warm place for about 10 minutes to activate into a foam.

Melt the butter in the milk while it scalds, and combine in a large mixing bowl with eggs, the remainder of the sugar, and salt. Add the milk last, gradually, while stirring constantly to keep the eggs from cooking. The mixture will have cooled to almost the proper temperature by the time the ingredients are combined. When it is lukewarm, add the yeast mixture and most of the flour.

I use a heavy earthenware bowl to knead dough. After oiling my hands, I close my fists and punch the dough in slow motion, lifting and turning it bottom side up during the process.

Use flour as needed, adding the final cup gradually to keep the dough from sticking to your hands. Keep your hands oiled while kneading. The dough should be as soft as can be handled. Knead until smooth and elastic, about 10 minutes. Cover the bowl with a damp cloth and set it in a warm place for the dough to rise. When double in bulk, punch the dough down, turn bottom side up, and allow to rise again.

During the first stage of my conversion, I substituted honey for the sugar and corn oil for the butter, saving out some of the corn oil to oil my hands while kneading. I also substituted ¾ cup of raw wheat germ and ¼ cup soya powder for one cup of the flour, and added ½ cup powdered milk. (Mix the wheat germ and the powdered soya and milk into two cups of the flour in a separate pan, and add this mixture to the other ingredients with the rest of the flour.)

Later, I devised a light dough with whole-grain wheat flour, which ordinarily has a tendency to bake a heavy loaf. Again, I found the secret to be the use of as little flour as possible to achieve a kneadable dough. When using the stone-ground whole wheat flour, I reduce the oil to ¼ cup and occasionally omit the wheat germ, since the flour is not devitalized. Or, I add about ¼ cup of wheat germ and make no other changes except in the quantity of flour used. Therafter, I proceed in the usual manner, except that after adding the yeast mixture I stir in about 6 cups of whole wheat flour to which I have added wheat germ, soya powder, and powdered milk, mixing well with a large spoon. Then I add more flour to make a dough stiff enough to stir for about 2 minutes.

After covering the dough and letting it rise for the first time, I punch it down for a second rising. After the second rising, I oil my hands two or three times and knead the dough until it is smooth and elastic.

One authority on baking bread suggests that soya powder and powdered milk be omitted by beginners baking with stone-ground whole-grain wheat flour. Both these ingredients lack gluten and may result in heavier loaves. Eggs may also be omitted and water may be substituted for milk.

Any of the following can be made with this dough, or you can create your own product. I usually bake a variety from one batch, including one of the breads or dinner rolls, perhaps a few cheese boats or hamburger wheels, and some kind of sweet roll.

BREAD LOAVES

For toast and sandwiches, make the loaves in bread pans. Brush loaves with evaporated milk and sprinkle with sesame or poppy seeds. Bake 1-pound loaves about 50 minutes, and larger loaves 70 minutes at 350°. To make round or oval loaves, shake cornmeal on a large baking pan, shape the dough, and place two loaves on each pan. Slash twice, brush tops with evaporated milk, and sprinkle on seeds. Bake at 350° for about 45 minutes. Let all loaves rise in a warm place before baking.

DINNER ROLLS

Any of the standard types of rolls can be made with this dough. I make a variety of shapes, including small braids, crescents, twists, and round rolls cut with a biscuit cutter. We like seeds on breads and rolls, so here again I brush with evaporated milk and sprinkle with seeds, then put the rolls aside to rise before baking at 350° for about 20 minutes.

FLATBREAD AND CRACKER BREAD

To make flatbread, roll pieces of dough about 1 inch thick into rounds the size of a dinner plate or smaller. The size is a matter of choice. Place on cookie sheets and puncture the rounds two or three times unless you want the two crusts to separate like Syrian bread. Brush with evaporated milk and sprinkle with seeds. Let rise in a warm place, then bake at 350° about 15 minutes on the bottom shelf of the oven and 15 minutes more on a higher shelf near the middle of the oven for even browning.

Follow the same procedure for cracker bread, but roll the dough as thin as piecrust or thinner. I make these rounds from 12 to 15 inches in diameter and use heavy foil ovenliners as baking pans. Roll the thin dough loosely on your rolling pin for easy transfer to ovenliners, then brush surface with evaporated milk and sprinkle on the seeds. Cracker bread does not have to rise again before baking.

Bake it at 350° for about 5 minutes on the bottom shelf of the oven, then bake about 7 minutes more on the higher shelf in the same manner as the flatbread. I put the thin rounds back in the warm oven after I have finished baking and let them dry to a brittle stage. In this dry stage, this bread will keep indefinitely in a dry place. I store mine in a large flat paper bag on top of our refrigerator. Gail's friends love this bread and often snap off pieces in passing, usually on their way out, since the refrigerator is by the back door.

I serve cracker bread, broken in pieces, instead of conventional crackers with hors d'oeuvres and usually have to replenish the tray several times. In damp weather, the bread can be crisped in a hot oven.

FRIED DOUGH

This novel use of yeast dough makes a big hit with everyone, especially children. Roll the dough thin. Cut it in squares or pinch off bits of dough and fry them in hot oil, turning once. Serve with a bowl of honey, maple syrup, jam, or jelly for dunking.

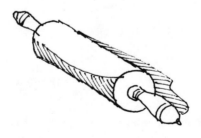

CHEESE BOATS
Penurli

A hot cheese boat, fresh out of the oven, is a rare treat. One of my cherished childhood recollections is running to the kitchen with my brothers and sister when my mother called to tell us the cheese boats were done.

Make this filling or devise your own combination, perhaps substituting cream cheese for cottage cheese:

1 egg, beaten	⅛ teaspoon paprika
½ cup cottage cheese	¼ pound shredded or
3 tablespoons fresh chopped	chopped mild cheese
parsley (or 1 tablespoon dried	some strong cheese or
parsley)	grated Parmesan cheese
salt and pepper to taste	

Measurements should not be rigid. I utilize leftover or dried-out cheese in this filling, too. Combine all ingredients in a bowl.

Roll out in piecrust-thin ovals of dough about 5 inches long and spread filling on them almost to the edge. Wet two small edge sections at the opposite ends of each oval, turn about one inch of the dry sections over the filling, and pinch the damp ends together into points, to give a boat shape. Lift with a spatula onto a baking sheet, placing the boats about one inch apart, and let rise. Bake at 350° about 20 minutes. Serve hot or reheat before serving.

If you decide to make cheese turnovers instead, place the filling on half of the oval, wet the edge of the dough, fold the other half over the filling, and seal the edges. Cut a hole in the top of each turnover for the steam to escape, brush with evaporated milk for a glossy finish, and let rise before baking.

HAMBURGER WHEELS

Create your own or try this filling:

1 pound lean ground beef or	4 tablespoons minced fresh
lamb	parsley (or 2 tablespoons dried
1 large chopped onion	parsley)
1 chopped green pepper	1 cup drained canned tomatoes
1 clove minced garlic	salt and pepper to taste

Make thin rounds of dough the size of a dinner plate or smaller, for the wheels. Slip dough onto a baking sheet or ovenliner and spread with meat mixture, turning a narrow one-inch edge over the meat. Bake as soon as possible after preparation in 350° oven for about 20 minutes.

For cheese buffs, try melting mild cheese over the filling before serving. I serve these hot as a main dinner course with soup and a green salad. They're good cold, too.

PIZZA

Make a base by draining canned tomatoes and blending in tomato paste for proper consistency. Add minced garlic, chopped green pepper, salt and pepper, and some chopped onion, or use a thick tomato spaghetti sauce for a base.

Roll out thin rounds of dough and brush with oil. Spread mild sliced cheese over the oil and cover with the tomato mixture. Sprinkle with oregano and grated Parmesan or Romano cheese. Slices of pepperoni, salami, mushrooms, and olives may be spread over the tomato mixture before baking on bottom shelf of a 350° oven about 20 minutes.

SWEET BREADS OR ROLLS

The variety here is endless. Use fresh, candied, or stewed dried fruits, jams, syrups, honey, berries, or nuts flavored with spices.

I usually roll out the dough into rectangles, spread them with soft butter or oil, sprinkle with spices, nuts, raisins, or dates, and roll up in the form of a jelly roll. Sometimes I transfer the roll to a pan, form it into a circle, and slash it into sections, turning each one on its side. Or I cut slices and arrange them, slightly apart, in a cake pan lined with honey and chopped nuts.

Once I covered the bottom of a pan with honey and fresh raspberries from our bushes. The rolls were delicious but the berries bubbled over into the oven. After that, I used either a larger pan or fewer berries. Another possibility is turnovers with berries, jam, or apple-raisin-spice filling.

The ice and snow came and cut off my only form of exercise—

walking. There wasn't enough snow for snowshoeing, so I put on boots, jacket, and a fur hat and started mushing down the road, walking on the low banks of snow the plow had pushed aside. But then I remembered the boys' sleds in the barn. I returned and dragged the larger one from the loft.

The road from our house to the Anderson home, where I have a standing invitation for hot coffee, is a series of downhill slopes. Why not bellyflop down? At the top of the first hill, I took a running start and flopped onto the sled as it hit the ground. I slid forward but the sled didn't. Picking myself up to analyze the situation, I figured that my weight pushed the sled into the packed snow and the rusty runners kept it from moving ahead, even downhill. So I returned to the barn and sanded the rust from runners, then retraced my steps to the hill.

This time, I decided to ride sitting on the sled. By pushing with my feet, I finally got going at a moderate pace. I really got a charge out of the ride. Unfortunately, the sled was not in condition to negotiate the smaller slopes so I still had to do a bit of walking. But I kept at it until the runners sharpened and I was able to ride most of the way.

Sometimes I wish we had lived here during the "good old days" when all the farm families got together on sleigh rides and tobogganing and skating parties. Those winter fun times died out when the farms were gradually sold to summer residents. When we first came twenty-seven years ago, we did manage to participate in the last cornhusking party and the last few square dances. Oh well, I'd probably fall apart square dancing now anyway ...

On the rare occasions when I make sour rye bread, I still combine the rye flour with unbleached white flour, as I have not experimented with using whole wheat flour with rye flour.

After Gail left home for college, George retired and I took a sedentary job for the first time. Both of us began to gain weight, so I stopped making sour rye bread. Bread and rolls made periodically from my basic yeast dough supply us amply with the little bread we eat while we struggle to keep within normal proportions.

For other homemakers who would like to experiment with rye and whole wheat flours, I suggest using ½ cup of gluten flour in the recipe since rye flour has very little gluten. Otherwise, a delicious but heavy loaf may result.

SOUR RYE BREAD

1 teaspoon honey or sugar	2 tablespoons caraway seeds
3 cups warm water	4 cups unbleached white flour
2 packages dry yeast	3½ cups rye flour
4 teaspoons salt	

Using a 2-cup measure, dissolve the honey or sugar in 1 cup of the warm water. Add the yeast and let stand a few minutes to activate into a foam.

Combine the remaining 2 cups of warm water, salt, caraway seeds, and white flour in a large mixing bowl. Beat well for 2 minutes; then add rye flour and more white flour, if necessary, for a medium-soft dough.

Knead with oiled hands until firm and smooth. Cover and let rise overnight in a warm place to sour the dough. Be sure the bowl is large enough to keep the dough from spilling over.

Shape in round or oval loaves on a flat pan sprinkled with cornmeal. Bake about 1 hour at 350° on the lower shelf of the oven. This recipe makes 4 small loaves. Try the bread toasted!

The following oatmeal bread recipe, which I recently concocted, turned out to be a winner. My family—and the guests who arrived as the loaves were cooling on a trivet—ate some and loved the flavor and texture. The inside was moist and tender and the outside, crusty and chewy. It is very easy to make, another attraction.

CRUSTY OATMEAL BREAD

2 cups quick rolled oats	1 package dry yeast softened in
2 cups boiling water	½ cup warm water
⅓ cup unsulfured molasses	5 cups flour (about)
1 tablespoon salt	4 tablespoons oil

Pour the boiling water over the oats. Add the molasses and salt. After cooling the mixture to lukewarm, add the softened yeast and water. Add enough flour for a medium-soft dough and knead well, oiling the hands with the measured oil.

Cover the dough and let it rise in a warm place until double in bulk. Then punch it down and form into two loaves. Brush the tops with evaporated milk and sprinkle with sesame or other seeds before letting rise again. Bake in 350° oven about 1 hour.

I used 1 cup whole wheat flour and the rest unbleached white flour, and coated the pan with cornmeal. After baking, tap the loaves out of the pans and cool on a trivet.

Years ago I found an easy way to make English muffins and gave out the recipe many times to the mothers of my children's friends, who snacked at our home on these toasted muffins spread with butter and homemade jam or marmalade. I always kept a supply in our freezer for this purpose.

As with my basic yeast dough, the English muffin recipe also went through three stages. Take your pick.

ENGLISH MUFFINS

1 or 2 packages dry yeast	1½ teaspoons salt
2 tablespoons sugar	2 tablespoons corn oil
½ cup warm water	4½ cups unbleached flour
1½ cups scalded milk	

Add sugar and yeast to warm water and set aside to activate. Scald the milk with the salt and oil and pour into a bowl. Cool to lukewarm, add yeast mixture, and stir in the flour. Cover the bowl and set in a warm place for the dough to rise. It will rise faster if 2 packages of yeast are used.

When I first fortified this recipe, I substituted ¼ cup raw wheat germ and one tablespoon soya powder for the same amount of flour, and blended ¼ cup powdered milk with the flour; I also substituted honey for the sugar. In the final version, I substituted 2 cups stone-ground whole wheat flour for the same amount of white flour.

Instead of rolling out the dough and going through all the rigamarole, I drop wads of dough on an ungreased griddle over medium-low heat and shape them into rounds about 1 inch thick with my fingers. The muffins should cook about 5 minutes on each side. Turn only once. Makes about 15 muffins. Refrigerate during warm weather; any extras can be frozen for later use.

March

OLD-TIMERS here say seeds for the summer garden should be started at town meeting time. Town meeting in this area is held the second Tuesday of March, so I try to get seeds into peat pots and flats by the middle of the month.

Usually I start with tomato, cucumber, pepper, zucchini, and broccoli seeds. Last year, I used some self-contained plant pots that resembled large checkers when I bought them in a farm supply store. Following the salesman's instruction, I soaked the disks in water and watched them swell into tiny pots. I planted one seed in each and in due time transferred the pots into the garden. I would have welcomed these disks a few years ago when I forgot to store soil for spring seedlings. That year I had to buy my plants.

An old bamboo bookstand with three shelves holds the peat pots and the self-contained pots in narrow trays. It is so gratifying to watch the seedlings grow in our porch greenhouse while the snows are still piled high outside.

This year I set weathered boards on bricks on the floor around the outside perimeter of the porch. Resting on the boards are pots of herbs intermingled with varieties of coleus, begonia, geranium, and other flowering plants. Hanging baskets drip with philodendron, fuchsia, and spider plants. Fortunately, the porch is huge, leaving room for a dining area, stereo, and my other interests. While I work, I like to listen to classical music. Current favorites are Tchaikovsky, Dvorak, and Rimsky-Korsakov.

Up here, March is still a rugged month, and nutritionists claim our resistance is at a low point because of the depletion of vitamins in winter-stored fruits and vegetables. Store-bought produce I consider inferior because it is sprayed with deadly insecticides and marketed weeks after picking; some vegetables are even coated with carcinogenic paraffin.

Wholesome grains in thick mushes, pilavs, and soups seem to fit well into menu planning for this cold period at the end of the winter. Many mushes begin with soup stock made with either a soupbone, chicken backs and necks, or saved bones, especially from roast turkey. After boiling with salt for several hours, strain cool stock and skim the fat off the top. Now the stock is ready for hearty soups, too.

Since soup stock is a perfect base for creative cooking, I merely offer suggestions instead of soup recipes. Try combining various grains with vegetables, starting with those that take longest to cook. If the soup seems too thin, thicken with a handful of fine noodles or vermicelli, both of which cook quickly. Flavor with spices, a lump of butter, cream, or milk. Try a dash of Worcestershire or soy sauce, too.

Among the grains, bulgur deserves more widespread use because of its versatility and nutrition. It is a form of cracked whole wheat used widely by Near Eastern nations and, I think, steadily gaining in popularity here. Another form of wheat that lends itself to many tasty grain dishes is hulled wheat, also known as hurled wheat. It looks somewhat like large barley but takes longer to cook.

These grains are not always easily available, but they can be found in Armenian, Greek, and health food stores and recently have become available through grain co-ops. I buy mine in quantity and freeze the excess amount during the summer, or leave it in the unheated utility room (formerly our woodshed) during the winter in tins, to foil the field mice that always manage to get in before winter.

Cooking frequently with whole grains will add variety, new flavors, and nutrition to help protect you against the expanding number of devitalized foods marketed each year. Our friends consider many of the grain dishes I serve gourmet foods. Some of them, like the pilavs, are simple to make; others require more dexterity.

I consider *koofta* tops in the creative group. Near Easterners have several versions, including a layered variety easier to make but harder to take on picnic lunches.

I did not learn to cook many of the Armenian dishes I knew as a child while my mother was alive, because she was an expert cook who later turned professional. We lived in the same house in Providence, and she often shared the foreign dishes she made; so I didn't bother learning, rationalizing that I had two small children and limited time. Anyhow, she usually chided me on the amateurish results of my rare attempts at the more intricate dishes and pastries, a good excuse to leave them to her. The only time I helped her make koofta, mine cracked while cooking.

One day while visiting at the farm, Mother insisted that I write down the recipe for the filling as I watched her put the whole thing together. She pointed out that she would not always be around to make koofta for us.

Years after her death, when George and I had a yen for koofta, I decided to try it again. I spent a whole afternoon going through a drawer full of recipes and notes until I found the yellowed sheet on which I had scribbled the recipe. I was fairly certain I could put the shell mixture together.

After a bit of experimenting, I feel I can now honestly say my koofta tastes as good as my mother's. It really isn't as much trouble to make as I imagined, either.

Near Eastern ethnic groups were lamb eaters, and my mother used lamb. She would buy a forequarter or leg and cut it up herself for several meals, all tasty and some time-consuming to prepare. She also ground the meat herself when necessary, and I still do, having inherited her meat grinder. Because lamb is too expensive sometimes—and not always readily available—I use ground lean chuck for the filling and a half-and-half mixture of ground lean chuck and lamb for the shell.

As I cut up a lamb leg for shish kebab, I put aside the less choice and slightly fatty pieces to grind for koofta meat. Lamb patties sold in markets are too fatty for koofta. Lamb shanks, if available, will do adequately if ground with lean chuck. Or use all ground chuck.

Save the shank bones to boil for the koofta broth. Call in a couple of neighbors or friends and make this a fun project of creativity in the kitchen. Buy fine bulgur for the shell; the coarse grind is used for pilavs.

For homemakers whose time is limited—and that includes me—the filling can be made a day or two in advance, since it must be cold before use.

KOOFTA FILLING

2 cups lean ground chuck
¼ cup corn oil
3 medium-large onions, chopped
⅓ cup chopped green pepper
½ cup chopped fresh parsley
  (or ¼ cup dried parsley flakes)
1 teaspoon salt
¼ teaspoon allspice

¼ teaspoon black pepper
½ cup pignolia nuts or any
  broken nut kernels
½ teaspoon paprika
⅛ teaspoon cinnamon
½ teaspoon dried basil
¼ teaspoon dried mint (optional)

In a large skillet sauté the meat and oil for about 5 minutes, stirring occasionally. Stir in the onions and cook 15 minutes. Add other ingredients and cook 5 minutes more; then chill.

KOOFTA SHELL

2 cups fine bulgur
cold water

2 cups lean ground chuck
salt and pepper to taste

Put the bulgur in a bowl and cover with water to an inch above the bulgur line. Let stand about 10 minutes for the water to absorb. Put the meat in a large bowl with room enough to knead, and add salt and pepper. Wash your hands. Take about ½ of the soaked bulgur and knead it into the meat by hand. Keep kneading and adding a little more water, alternately with the rest of the bulgur, until the mixture is the consistency of soft dough.

Arrange all the ingredients on a table, along with a sheet of wax paper and a bowl of water. Wet palms of the hands, take a lump of the shell mixture, and roll it into a ball the size of a Ping-Pong ball or a little larger. Insert thumb of the right hand in the center of the ball, and roll the ball in the left hand into a hollow like a cup. Insert some filling, pinch the shell together, wet hands again and pat the shell into a flat round in the palms.

If the shell mixture becomes stiff—and it is likely to until one gains speed in shaping—knead it again with a little water. I have cut my time in half, but still find I must knead once in between. The trick is to make the walls as thin as possible and still get in the most filling. Set each koofta on wax paper. Bring strained broth made from the bones to a boil, or make broth with bouillon cubes. Boil 4 or 5 kooftas at a time, without crowding, for 10 minutes. Remove each batch with a slotted spoon. So some of them are cracked—they will still taste good, and you'll do better next time. This recipe makes 25 to 30 kooftas.

Kooftas may be served hot, with or without broth, or eaten cold. They are great on picnics! They freeze without broth very well and can be thawed quickly in hot broth. Do not store them in broth; keep broth and koofta separate. I don't know why. I was told not to and never questioned it. I usually have filling left over, which I also freeze in a plastic container.

A dandy way to serve plain, unfilled kooftas, which are shaped slightly thicker than hamburgers, is to split each, dip in beaten egg, and fry in butter over low heat. Serve with a salad for a fine luncheon dish. Include hot rolls, if desired.

To make an easy version of filled kooftas, which probably would be best at first, butter or oil an 8 x 12 inch pan with sides or one of similar size. Divide the shell mixture in half and spread a layer in the bottom of the pan. Cover this with filling and top with the rest of the shell mixture. Cut in diamonds, using a knife blade dipped in water; dot each piece generously with butter, and sprinkle 3 tablespoons of water over all. Bake at 350° for 30 minutes. Serves 4 to 6 persons.

Bulgur pilavs, using the coarse grind, can be made in several variations, all good. A heavy utensil with a tight cover should be used for all pilavs. I also inherited my mother's pilav pot with a glass-domed lid through which I can observe without lifting. Pilavs should be uncovered as little as possible while cooking.

One-fourth cup yellow split peas may be substituted for the same amount of bulgur for a subtle, different flavor. For another variation, substitute canned tomatoes for part of the broth.

BASIC BULGUR PILAV

½ cup butter or oil
¼ cup vermicelli, crumbled
1 onion, chopped

1½ cups coarse bulgur
3 cups hot chicken or meat broth
salt and pepper to taste

Over high heat, combine butter or oil or a mixture of both, vermicelli, and onion in the pilav pot. Sauté, stirring constantly, until vermicelli cooks to a light tan color. Quickly stir in the bulgur until each grain is coated. Add broth, salt and pepper, and cover. When the pot boils, lower heat and let simmer until the liquid is absorbed—about 20 minutes. Makes 4 to 6 servings.

To make an herb pilav, omit the vermicelli and cut the broth to 2½ cups. Add ¼ cup fresh or frozen parsley, one chopped green pepper, one chopped stalk of celery, ¼ teaspoon dried or several leaves of chopped fresh basil, the same amount of dill ferns, and a little sage with the broth. Try other herbs, too. This is my favorite bulgur pilav but George likes the plain version. I usually make the herb pilav when fresh herbs are available.

For a bulgur pilav with greens, add 2 cups of cut chard, spinach, beet, or other greens to the basic pilav with the broth. Bits of leftover meat will give it added flavor. Almost anything goes in pilavs. Water may be used instead of broth. Better still, increase the flavor with bouillon cubes.

BASIC RICE PILAV

½ cup butter or oil
¼ cup pignolia nuts or
    other broken nut kernels
¼ cup vermicelli, crumbled

1¼ cups long-grain raw rice
3 cups chicken broth
salt and pepper to taste

Over high heat, sauté vermicelli and nuts in butter or oil or a mixture of both until the vermicelli turns a light tan color. Stir in rice until each grain is coated. Add broth, season with salt and pepper, cover and proceed as for bulgur pilav.

Chicken fat is often used as part of the fat mixture. If brown rice is used, a little more broth may be necessary as brown rice takes longer to cook. Thin spaghetti may be substituted for vermicelli. Nuts are optional, but give pilav a gourmet touch. Use chicken bouillon cubes with water if broth is not available. I always use chicken broth for rice pilav rather than meat stock, and often serve it with chicken. Makes 4 to 6 servings.

To make a seafood pilav, sauté a large chopped onion instead of the vermicelli and use clam broth and water for the liquid, adding chopped clams, lobster, or other seafood with the liquid.

A pilav similar to Spanish rice can be made by sautéing a chopped green pepper with the onion, and using canned tomatoes for part of the liquid. Try a variation of your own.

Combinations of grain, herbs, and sometimes meat and vegetables make really hearty cold-weather mushes with subtle Old World flavors. The healthy Old Country folks included a salad, fruit, cheese and bread for a nutritious meal. Experiment a little with combinations of various grains. However, some take longer to cook than others so should be worked into recipes at different times. Go easy on herbs and spices until experience teaches you to judge the right amounts to use. So you make a few mistakes. How else does one learn?

Now that George and I are alone most of the time, we have rediscovered the superior flavors of simpler foods, eaten in moderation, and these grain dishes are favored. I use imported red lentils but regular lentils can be used. Cook the following recipes in heavy pots, preferably stainless steel, stirring frequently to prevent sticking.

HERBED LENTIL AND BULGUR MUSH

Vospov Aboor

1 large onion, chopped	1 stalk celery, chopped
4 tablespoons butter and oil mixed	½ cup fresh or frozen chopped parsley
2 quarts soup stock or water	6 leaves fresh basil, chopped (or
¾ cup lentils	½ teaspoon dried basil)
½ cup coarse bulgur	salt and pepper to taste
1 green pepper, diced	

In a heavy pot sauté the onions in the butter mixture for about 5 minutes. Add other ingredients and cook until lentils and bulgur are soft, about 30 minutes. Add more water or stock if necessary, but retain the consistency of a fairly thick mush and stir often to prevent sticking. Serves 4 to 6 persons, depending on whether this, like other mushes, is the main meal with salad, cheese, fruit, and bread or whether it is served as a side dish. Mushes freeze well, so I keep an extra quantity in the freezer for unexpected guests.

SPICED MEAT AND WHEAT MUSH

Keshkeg

Here is another tasty one-dish grain meal that needs only a salad for complete gustatory satisfaction. Extremely easy to make, it must be eaten to be appreciated. Do not try to judge it by reading the recipe. Make it.

1½ quarts chicken or meat broth	¼ teaspoon paprika
1 cup hulled wheat	¼ to ½ teaspoon ground
2 cups cooked ground chicken	fenugreek or curry
or meat	salt and pepper to taste
4 tablespoons butter or half oil	

Use a fowl if possible, so that good broth will be available too. Combine broth and wheat in a heavy pot and simmer until wheat is soft and most of liquid absorbed, about 1½ hours. Stir occasionally to keep from sticking and add more broth during cooking if necessary. Add the other ingredients to make a thick mushy mixture and cook 15 minutes more. Continue stirring often. Serve in deep dishes, adding a lump of butter to each serving. Makes 4 to 6 servings.

GRAINS AND GREENS MUSH

Panjar Aboor

¼ cup dry chick-peas	½ cup hulled wheat
1 chopped onion	1 cup lentils
4 tablespoons butter or half oil	1 package frozen greens (or
2 quarts water	2 cups cooked fresh greens)

Soak chick-peas overnight. Sauté onions in butter or butter and oil combination for about 5 minutes. Add water, wheat, drained chick-peas, and cook about 1 hour. Add lentils and greens. Allow to simmer, stirring frequently, until grains are soft, about 30 minutes more. Add more water if necessary. Season with salt and pepper. Makes 4 to 6 servings.

HULLED WHEAT WITH YOGURT

Ton Aboor

½ cup hulled wheat
1½ cups water
1 egg, beaten

1 pint plain yogurt
butter
mint

Cook wheat in enough water until soft and water is absorbed, about
1½ hours. Beat egg and yogurt together, and heat in the top of a
double boiler to prevent yogurt from curdling. Work some of the
yogurt mixture into the wheat gradually, to avoid lumping; then
combine in the double boiler. Season with salt and add fresh chopped
or crushed dry mint to taste. Start with 4 leaves of fresh mint or ¼
teaspoon dry. More yogurt may be added to get a looser mixture.
Measurements need not be rigid in these recipes. Serve each portion
hot with a lump of butter swirled through.
    Served cold without butter, this dish is refreshing in hot weather.
Omit egg, as yogurt need not be heated. Cool wheat after cooking
and gradually work in the yogurt. Makes 2 to 4 servings.

RICE WITH YOGURT

Matzoonov Josh

1 egg
1 pint plain yogurt
½ cup raw white or brown rice

1 cup boiling water
salt to taste
butter

Beat egg and yogurt together and heat in top of a double boiler.
Cook rice in water, adding a little more water if brown rice is used.
Combine rice with yogurt mixture, season, and serve with a lump of
butter in each bowl. Serves 2 or more.

TOP-OF-STOVE RICE PUDDING

Gatnaboor

1 quart of milk
⅓ cup white or brown rice
¼ cup honey or sugar

⅛ teaspoon salt
¼ cup raisins (optional)
spices

Bring milk to a boil in the top of a double boiler. Add other
ingredients, stir until the mixture boils again, and cook covered over

hot water until the rice is soft. Pour into pudding dishes and dust with a mixture of cinnamon, nutmeg, and allspice, or just one of these spices. Makes 6 to 8 servings.

As most of my friends know, I am a rather gullible person. On the rare occasions when I visit health food stores, proprietors find me easy prey to sell new items that are conducive to good health.

One day I bought millet, which then got stored in the utility room refrigerator for a year. When I finally decided it was time to try cooking some, I investigated the nutritional value of this grain. Through different sources, I learned that it is high in natural protein and lecithin. It is also particularly high in vitamin B-2 and minerals, including magnesium, potassium, silicon, iron, calcium, and phosphorus. This seed has an alkaline ash and is easily digested.

Millet, I learned too, is among the most ancient of grains. It was grown in prehistoric times and generally used during Biblical times and before, in some parts of the world.

I cooked it several ways and found it delicious in addition to all that nutrition. The only drawback to this searching for and sharing nutritional recipes, however, is a losing battle of the bulge. I suppose it's an occupational hazard. If I could only stop with a taste. But no— I keep on eating until my diet goes down the drain! I make more fresh starts than anyone I know.

MILLET PILAV

3 tablespoons corn oil	2 cups water
1 cup millet	salt and pepper

Heat oil in a heavy skillet, add the millet, and stir about 2 minutes to coat and slightly toast each seed. Add the water and seasoning. Cover tightly, lower heat, and let simmer after it boils until the water is absorbed and the millet is fluffy. Millet pilav is very good with the meat course. Next time I shall sprinkle it with chopped parsley and perhaps a little dill. Makes about 3 servings.

Here is a dandy pudding. It is a little too sweet for my taste, so I spoon unsweetened thawed strawberries over it and can eat almost a whole batch!

MILLET PUDDING

2½ cups milk
¼ cup honey
½ cup millet meal
2 eggs, beaten

½ teaspoon vanilla
¼ cup unsweetened coconut
(optional)

I had planned to make this pudding with whole millet seed, when I remembered my twenty-five-cent coffee grinder, the one I got at the rummage sale. I decided to grind the seeds for a smoother pudding.

Heat 2 cups of the milk in the top of a double boiler with the honey. Stir the rest of the cold milk into the millet meal, then add the hot milk. Let cook over hot water about 30 minutes, stirring occasionally. Add a little of the hot pudding to the eggs gradually; then pour the egg mixture into the double boiler and cook about 5 minutes more. Remove from heat and stir in the vanilla and coconut. Pour the pudding in individual glasses and dust with powdered cardamon seed if desired. Makes about 4 servings.

MILLET CEREAL

½ cup milk
1 cup water
¼ teaspoon salt

½ cup millet
1 tablespoon honey or sugar
raisins or dried fruit (optional)

Combine milk, water, and salt in the top of a double boiler. Bring to boil over direct heat and gradually add the millet. Boil about 5 minutes, stirring occasionally; then cook over boiling water for 30 minutes. Add fruit and honey, and cook 5 minutes longer. Makes 1 to 2 servings.

Since we are on grains, here is a gem I put together for the benefit of children, as well as all those interested in a good breakfast cereal at a reasonable cost. It is loaded with vitamins and minerals, far better than most cereals bought in stores. I call it:

HIGH-NUTRITION DRY CEREAL

8 cups rolled oats
4 cups raw wheat germ
1 cup sesame seed
2 cups shredded coconut
¼ cup millet

1 cup sunflower seed kernels
(optional)
2 teaspoons cinnamon
1 cup honey
⅔ cup corn oil

raisins and nuts

Combine all the ingredients except the honey, oil, raisins, and nuts, and mix in a large bowl to distribute evenly. Wash your hands, and use your fingers to work in the honey and the oil. Spread the mixture on flat pans and bake in a 300° oven for 20 minutes, stirring a few times while baking. Cool, and add raisins and nuts. Store in an airtight container in a cool place. I use unsweetened coconut but sweetened is all right. Use toasted wheat germ if you are unable to buy it raw. Serve as a dry snack or in a cereal bowl with milk, fresh berries, or sliced bananas. Makes about 5 quarts. You can make ½ the recipe if desired.

If you are not familiar with the soybean (I'm a recent convert), let me introduce you to this excellent food now. After investigation into its nutritional value, I am convinced more homemakers would include it in family menus if they would taste it once.

This bean is extra rich in protein, superior in flavor and texture over other beans, and versatile as well. To take full advantage of it, I cook extra in advance and leave it in a bowl in the refrigerator, handy to be added to soups, salads, and other foods, including meat loaves.

Although I bought a couple of pounds of soybeans two years ago, for a long time I never cooked any, probably because (with the exception of soybean loaf) no one I knew seemed to have a good, easy recipe. After the recent disclosures on the bad effects of stilbestrol injection in beef, poultry, and other meats, and the high price of meats, I took a second look at soybeans and learned that for the price of rib roast, I could get 30 pounds of them!

The soybeans would furnish 12 times more protein than the roast, 126 times more calcium, 18 times more phosphorus, 17 times more iron, 60 times more vitamin B-1, 12 times more vitamin B-2, and more than 15,000 international units of vitamin A, not found in the beef. The soybean is also rich in lecithin and contains all the essential amino acids. According to the U.S. Department of Health, Education and Welfare, "The soybean is in so many respects the most valuable of all plant foods."

That did it! I started experimenting, and devised these excellent recipes.

SOYBEANS AND CHICK-PEAS

Combine 1 cup soybeans and ½ cup chick-peas in a pan of water and soak them overnight. (Since soybeans take a long time to cook, I figured they should combine well with dry chick-peas, which also must cook a long time.)

Drain the beans and peas the next morning. Then barely cover them with fresh water, add salt, put a lid on the pot, bring to a boil, and let simmer until the beans are cooked. Drain and serve with fresh-ground pepper. Delicious! Try some with a little butter too. Again, delicious!

Here are more goodies from this base.

SOYBEANS AND FRIED ONIONS

Slice one or two onions in a generous amount of a combination of butter and corn oil, and cook. When the onions are done, add cooked soybeans and chick-peas, or only soybeans. Stir, heat through, and season. The quantities are a matter of taste. I go easy on the fat combination because of my perennial weight problem.

SOYBEAN SALAD

To a quart of cooked soybeans (or a combination of soybeans and other beans), add the desired amount of raw onion rings, fresh or frozen parsley and dill, chopped celery, minced garlic or garlic powder, seasoning, and oil and vinegar (2 parts oil to 1 part vinegar). Add cherry tomatoes or cut-up tomatoes if desired. Serve on lettuce or romaine. Makes 5 servings.

SOYBEANS AND SNOW PEAS

Sauté 2 slivered onions in a large skillet with oil or butter or a mixture of both, about 2 tablespoons, for 2 minutes. Add 1 quart of edible pod snow peas and only enough water to keep the peas from sticking to the pot while they steam, about ½ cup. Cover and simmer until the peas are barely cooked. Do not overcook. Add 2 cups cooked soybeans, 2 tablespoons soy sauce, and salt and pepper to taste. Stir, heat through, and serve.

If snow peas are not available, try other vegetables such as green beans, broccoli, even greens. Be creative! Cut other quantities in half if using a package of commercially frozen vegetables, or use two packages of the frozen. Makes 4 to 6 servings.

SOYBEANS WITH HARD-BOILED EGGS

Combine chopped hard-boiled eggs and soybeans in any quantity desired. Add chopped onions, parsley, green pepper, and a little dill fern, salt, pepper, and paprika. Bind with a little mayonnaise and serve on lettuce or other greens. This is a fine hot weather meal with fruit, crackers or rolls, and cheese.

SOYBEANS WITH NUTS

Sauté 2 cups cooked soybeans in butter until heated through. Add ½ cup chopped nuts, salt to taste, and sauté 5 minutes more. Substitute for the "meat" dish in a meal.

The soybean pièce de résistance, I discovered, is baked soybeans. I decided to try them one day without telling George, who would eat baked beans three times a day if I served them. He never knew the difference—he thought he was eating baked pea beans. When I reheated some of the baked soybeans the next day, I noticed that these beans stayed whole and did not get mushy like other baked beans.

BAKED SOYBEANS

3 cups soybeans	2 teaspoons salt
½ cup unsulfured molasses	1 teaspoon dry mustard
⅓ cup corn oil	1 large onion

Soak the beans overnight with water to cover. Drain, add fresh water to cover, and boil for 1 hour or longer, skimming the foam as it forms. Pour into a bean pot, with cooking liquid slightly below the level of the beans. Mix in the molasses, oil, salt, and dry mustard. Cut the onion in chunks and press these down into beans. Bake all day.

About 1 pound of salt pork can be used instead of oil. Being health-conscious, I try to stay away from animal fats.

To tell the truth, the last time I made these beans I did not bake them. After combining the ingredients in a heavy stainless steel covered pan, I let them simmer from 10 A.M. to 7 P.M. on the stove burner, then served them with ketchup and homemade relish. Makes 1½ quarts of beans. You may want to cut this recipe in half. I froze the extra quantity.

I met a couple one day who had been eating soybean frankfurters they said could not be distinguished from the so-called "meat" frank-

furters, so I decided to do some experimenting and see if I could fool
Gail and George into thinking they were eating spiced hamburgers
instead of soyburgers. They weren't fooled, but they admitted the
soyburgers were tasty both with ketchup and as soy cheeseburgers.
I thought they were great! I made extra patties and froze them with
plastic wrap between, for easy separation.

SOYBEAN PATTIES

2 cups mashed cooked soybeans	1 teaspoon each salt and paprika
1 or 2 eggs	½ teaspoon each curry powder,
1 green pepper, chopped	sage, black pepper, and
1 kernel garlic, minced	celery salt
2 tablespoons corn, peanut, or	
other oil	

Combine all ingredients, form into 5 patties, and cook over a slow
fire in an oiled skillet.

Sap buckets will be hanging from the maple trees here soon, herald-
ing the beginning of the maple syrup season. We developed a taste
for this delicacy the first year we came, when ours was the only farm
without buckets hanging from the trees.

One year when the boys were about ten and twelve years old, they
decided to get into the act. After much slave labor before and after
school collecting sap, and boiling it outside on an old fireplace on
weekends, they ended up with one quart of syrup of dubious quality.
One huge enamel caldron, once my mother-in-law's, was blackened
beyond redemption.

After that we bought syrup, except for one year a neighboring
farmer offered me some half-boiled sap at a low price. Never one to
pass up a bargain, especially since money was the scarce commodity
here then, I took the sap home in a large milk can.

Vaguely I remembered the boys had boiled the sap outside and that
most of the farmers had a sap house for this operation. Something
about the sticky vapor ... No matter. I dug out my biggest pots and
filled three, putting them on both my stoves to boil. At that time in
addition to an electric stove, I had a two-burner oil cooking stove,
which George and the boys later took to the dump one day when I
wasn't home. I was heartbroken; I felt I needed that stove, with all
the canning and other cooking projects I was always getting involved
in. Besides, it sat under the window with the mountain view, and in

early spring I could watch the sun set behind the mountains as I cooked dinner.

Back to the syrup boiling tranquilly on both stoves: I went into the kitchen periodically, checked and tasted the syrup, and found nothing amiss. Near the end of the afternoon I was mentally congratulating myself on my business acumen as I washed pint jars in which to seal the syrup. Wouldn't everyone be pleased when they returned home from school and work to see my bargain bounty!

Once the jars were ready I drew a glass of water, and as I was drinking it, I glanced up. The kitchen walls and ceiling were covered with tiny brown beads! Frantically I ran around slamming shut all the doors leading out of the kitchen—in most instances too late. At first, in my panic, I had also shut off the fires, but decided that was like shutting the barn door after the horse escaped, so I turned them on again.

When I calmed down enough to think straight, I wet a large sponge, climbed up on my small ladder, and started sponging down the ceiling and walls. I had planned to repaper and paint anyway. I just got to it a little sooner.

MAPLE NUT AND SEED SQUARES

2 eggs, separated	⅛ teaspoon salt
½ cup maple syrup	½ cup nuts, broken in pieces
½ cup flour	¼ cup sesame seeds (optional)

Beat the egg yolks until light. Add the syrup, flour, and salt. Beat the egg whites until stiff, and fold them in along with the broken nutmeats and seeds. Pour the batter into an oiled square pan and bake at 350° for about 20 minutes. Delicious with a scoop of ice cream or some other such embellishment. Makes about 4 servings.

I use stone-ground whole wheat flour for this recipe. Sometimes I substitute honey for the syrup, since maple syrup is not as plentiful these days.

Here is a yummy dessert I concocted, which should make it easier to get children to eat cereal and eggs.

MAPLE NUT DESSERT

1 cup farina or cream of wheat	3 or 4 eggs (separated)
1 cup water	½ cup raisins
⅓ cup butter or corn oil	½ cup chopped nuts
1 teaspoon baking powder	1 cup maple syrup

Cook the cereal with water for the length of time suggested on the box. Stir in the butter, baking powder, egg yolks, raisins, and nuts after mixture has cooled a little, to prevent the egg yolks from cooking. Fold in the egg whites, stiffly beaten, and pour into an 8 x 12 inch pan. Bake at 350° for 30 to 40 minutes. Remove from the oven and cut in squares. Pour the maple syrup over the hot dessert and let it stand for an hour or two until the syrup is absorbed. Serve with ice cream, whipped cream, and more syrup if desired.

I sometimes use honey instead of syrup and peanuts instead of other nuts. Give this dish your own touch, perhaps by adding spices. Serves 4 to 6 persons.

We have two fat cats, both male, and both about as useful as lumbago. They sit around all day waiting for George to overfeed them. Periodically, they work up enough energy to fight with each other. They live in and under our barn. They know "Here kitty, kitty" usually means dinner is served, so will appear at the call.

During my walks, one or the other, whichever one sees me first, will accompany me, annoying me by getting underfoot. Sometimes neither one will notice my appearance and I can take off alone. After a late snowfall one day, I went for a short walk alone and was returning up our driveway when I noticed a mole against the white snow.

I called the cats and both dashed out of the barn, positioned so that the mole was between us. They both stopped and watched the mole slither toward the house, then ran toward me, looking for something to eat. I hastily tried to pick one up and drop him on the mole which was resting against the house foundation, but both cats suddenly suspicious of my intentions, dashed away from me. Giving up in exasperation, I went on into the house, chagrined to realize that George would never let them get hungry enough to hunt.

April

SPRING remains my favorite season because of the rebirth of nature. Even I revive.

We open only the screened sliding doors on the porch, to foil the wasps, which are already astir. The only sound outside is the song of birds. I hear a phoebe and a redwing blackbird in the swale. Nuthatches and chickadees are silently pecking at the two net bags of suet hanging from the yellow plum tree by the porch. My bucolic reverie is broken by the sound of a passing auto . . .

The melting snow had revealed the mounds of garbage on our garden plot, so George and I took advantage of a lovely Easter Sunday to bury them. This was the accumulation of the winter, when we are forced to bury garbage in the snow until it can later be turned underground to add organic material to our rich soil and give the worms a treat. The garden was full of worms, squirming with delight. I recognized most as descendants of a hybrid variety I had raised. Mine were a deeper shade of pink with a distinct band around their middles.

Witchgrass had worked its way into a thick bunch of chives in the herb garden, so I dug up and pulled apart the tiny oniony bulbs, already shooting up bright green spears. Working outside the first few times always helps erase the apathy I am plagued with during the winter. My bones creak a bit and my muscles protest, but I'll overcome this with more exercise.

I pruned one of the two grapevines emerging from the snow by the stone wall, but the other one is still partially buried where the snow drifted against the wall and froze. It is melting fast, we note happily.

On the porch, the tomato and pepper seedlings and other plants in peat pots and the self-contained pots are waiting to be transplanted to the garden. The large gizmo planter is choked with cherry tomato plants hanging with clusters of fruit, providing us with fresh tomatoes in the salad bowl. Ah, such a rare treat, and so much appreciated.

I took inventory of our Jerusalem artichoke plot, to find that a few mice had wintered under the mulch hay and gnawed at some of the tubers. We had harvested most of them last fall, so I was anxious to know if enough roots were left to replenish our supply. My digging fork struck treasure—enough tubers to fill my pail, some barely sprouting, most crisp and delicious. Cutting them up like seed potatoes, I replanted half of my find and refrigerated the remaining hoard for eating.

I was introduced to this superb vegetable through reading about its nutritive value. Unable to find seeds or roots to plant, I discovered a package of the tubers for sale one winter on the vegetable counter of a supermarket, and planted one of them in a windowbox of herbs in our living room. (We didn't have the porch then.) That tuber grew straight up and threatened to go through the ceiling, and I had to stake it carefully. As soon as the frost was out of the ground, I dug a plot away from our garden and planted it, cutting the stem back to about one foot. It took hold and spread, one reason why it is advisable to find a new plot, rather than let the plant invade an established garden area.

We ate most of that first harvest raw. I had every intention of trying some cooked, but got only as far as successfully substituting a few for water chestnuts in one recipe and slicing some in one of my low-cal vegetable combinations, cooked al dente like Chinese vegetables. Mostly, we shredded the raw tubers in coleslaw and other vegetable salads and used some cut up with other vegetables, as snacks on our periodic reducing diets.

The Jerusalem artichoke has a crisp texture and bland, slightly nutty flavor. It contains very little starch in the form of inulin, is easy to digest, and filling. This vegetable is not a true artichoke but a member of the sunflower family. The stalks are almost identical to and as tall as the sunflower's, but the flowers are much smaller. They are lovely in bouquets. I hope we always have enough of this fine vegetable to share with field mice.

Here is a recipe for serving the artichokes cooked, for all who can eat butter without a guilty feeling.

HOT BUTTERED JERUSALEM ARTICHOKES

Wash 1½ pounds artichokes, then steam them or drop into boiling water. To prevent discoloration, add 1 teaspoon vinegar or white wine. Cook, covered, only until tender. If permitted to cook beyond that point, they will again become tough. Test with a toothpick after 15 minutes. Drain, and remove skin.

Melt 2 to 3 tablespoons of butter; add 2 drops hot pepper sauce and 2 tablespoons chopped parsley, and pour over the artichokes. Makes 4 to 5 servings. (Artichokes can also be served in a cream sauce.)

After eating these artichokes cooked, I developed an urge to duplicate Johnny Appleseed's feat, traversing the countryside and planting Jerusalem artichokes instead of apple seed. Euell Gibbons, in *Stalking the Wild Asparagus,* says this tuber can be cooked and mashed with butter like mashed potatoes, but will not have the smooth texture. He also lists a recipe for Jerusalem artichoke chiffon pie and, like me, has sliced some raw into salads. His personal choice, he claims, is to arrange peeled Jerusalem artichokes around a roast and let them cook in the gravy with the meat.

I was very pleased with the result of this recipe that I concocted using four tubers about the size of large lemons.

SKILLET ARTICHOKES

Combine 4 peeled artichokes, sliced, and 1 large thinly sliced onion in a large skillet with 2 tablespoons of corn oil. Sauté for about 5 minutes and add ¼ cup water, salt, and pepper. Cover and simmer until cooked. Makes 3 servings.

George and I spent one afternoon pruning the raspberries, emerging with scratched wrists and ankles. Although we wore gloves, we know now we should have added puttees and worn longer sleeves.

In spite of drawing blood, I enjoyed every minute among the thorny canes, although I grieved for the bedraggled condition of the patch. The snows really raised havoc in that area. We pruned and propped up most of the canes. Many were flat on the ground. Others were leaning over on the point of collapse. I was in the same condition the next morning. However, we all revived in a couple of days.

Our raspberry patch hasn't needed thinning for the past four years, since the moles selected it for their annual convention. Every spring we stomp through the patch closing the tunnels, which aerate the roots of the canes and finally kill some.

I have tried various methods of coping with this problem, to no avail. The last one, which looked good to me, was to install small windmills throughout. The fellow who found this successful discovered accidentally that his lawn decoration discouraged moles when the spinning blades created a vibration underground. He said all his moles moved to his neighbor's property, until his neighbor got wise and installed windmills too.

I was going to try it, but gave up after spending all year trying to get someone to build me small windmills. Recently I heard of another surefire method that I could handle myself—burying empty bottles with their necks exposed to catch the wind in the infested area. The resulting resonance is supposed to scare the moles away.

Having no empty small bottles, I walked the roadside, usually full of discards from litterers. Just because I was looking for them this time, all I found was two beer bottles and one soda bottle. I buried them in the raspberry patch. I need more but will get them from our friends, Richard and Shirley Thorne, who have a summer farm down the road. They promised to save their bottles for me.

It was Sunday and raining again. I decided to take the chill out of the house and at the same time get a lift with creative baking, settling on my simplified method of making one version of the famous Near Eastern dessert—paklava.

This seemed an opportune time to try out the hollow plastic rolling pin Judy and Babe gave me on my last birthday. It can be filled with hot water to facilitate rolling out a thin dough. In the past, I had discovered that a metal table and metal rolling pin on a cold day made rolling out a thin dough almost impossible. A wooden rolling pin and surface are a better combination, if a hollow plastic rolling pin is not available, for making this pastry.

Before you start, buy a ½-inch, 3-foot wooden dowel, sold in most hardware stores. Wash it and rub vegetable oil into the raw wood.

Another ingredient you will need is a box of cooking cornstarch, to be used instead of flour to roll out the dough.

Most homemakers who make paklava buy phyllo sheets of the tissue-paper-thin dough to make this dessert. I start from scratch and make the phyllo pastry. Instead of using layers of the thin sheets, I roll each nut-filled sheet into an accordion, the version called *dolangar* or *boorma*.

Traditionally sugar syrup is used, but since I use honey or maple syrup, I call the dessert

MAPLE-NUT ACCORDIONS

2 cups unsifted flour	2 teaspoons corn oil
2 teaspoons baking powder	1 tablespoon honey or sugar
½ teaspoon salt	⅓ cup water (about)
1 egg	

Combine the dry ingredients and stir with a fork. Beat the egg with the remaining ingredients; then add to the dry ingredients and knead for a couple of minutes. The dough should be medium soft. If it is too stiff, add a little more water.

Put the dough in a bowl and cover with a damp cloth. Set aside in a warm place to rest while you prepare the nut filling.

NUT FILLING

4 ounces nutmeats	3 tablespoons brown sugar (or 2 tablespoons granulated sugar)

Pulverize the nuts by grating, bashing with the rolling pin, or stomping. If I have no shelled hickory nuts or butternuts, I use walnuts. (Most food stores carry 4-ounce cans of shelled walnuts. I usually keep a couple on hand for emergencies. Grated nuts can be bought in plastic bags or buy broken nut pieces.) Add sugar to the pulverized nuts, stir, and put aside.

Now we're ready: Roll the dough in a rope and cut it into 15 pieces. Each will be about the size of a golf ball. Shape each into a ball and return all to the bowl under the damp towel.

Shake cornstarch generously on your rolling surface. Roll out one of the balls as thin as possible with the rolling pin. Cover the surface of this thin sheet with more cornstarch and wrap the edge of it over the 3-foot wooden dowel, which has also been rubbed with cornstarch.

Roll up the entire sheet of dough on the dowel, using both hands to work the dowel back and forth as you roll with some pressure, causing the sheet to thin out still more as you roll it up. Does that make sense? It is difficult to explain, so experiment a little. Be generous with the cornstarch or you will never be able to unroll the thinned sheet. Keep rolling until the sheet is as thin as you can get it.

I remember my mother rolling out several rounds the size of dinner plates, stacking one on top of the other after covering each with cornstarch, then rolling them all at once with the dowel and, finally, peeling the tissue-thin sheets apart. The one time I tried it, they all stuck together because I used too little cornstarch. Now I take a little longer and do one at a time.

When you finally have a thin sheet, shake off the extra cornstarch and brush the entire surface with a mixture of warm melted butter and oil. Place a 1-inch-wide strip of the pulverized nut mixture horizontally across the center of the sheet.

Using the dowel, begin at the front edge and roll the oiled sheet and nuts loosely on the dowel, then press each outside edge of the cylinder of dough toward the center, forming an accordion. Slip the dowel out.

Arrange the accordions in rows in a heavily oiled or buttered 8 x 12 x 2 inch pan. (If all the pieces do not fit into the oblong pan, put the extras in another small pan, well oiled or buttered.) Brush the tops generously with more of the warm butter and oil mixture, and bake in a 350° oven, on the middle shelf, until golden—about 30 minutes. Cool on a trivet and serve with maple syrup or honey.

George likes this dessert soaked in the syrup. I prefer it crisp, with the syrup poured on at eating time. It's a matter of opinion.

I also make this pastry in a round pan with 2-inch sides, about the size of a pizza pan, putting the accordions end to end in a spiral.

My chief problem now is to find spots to plant five more fruit trees and six bush cherries when they arrive. George leaves such decisions to me; then if the locations prove unsatisfactory in later years, I will have no one else to blame. I must decide soon so that George can dig holes to receive them.

Early in the spring, I ordered two mulberry trees, two apricot trees, and one Chinese date, whatever that is. According to the seed catalogue, these trees are hardy and will survive our winters.

My reasoning in planting mulberries is that the birds will be attracted to the mulberries and leave the other fruit and berries alone. We'll harvest any mulberries they leave. I haven't seen a bearing mulberry tree since my sons were toddlers and we picked ripe berries from an Italian neighbor's huge tree. We ate them in quantity and made jam, too.

The flavor and versatility of cabbage make it one of my favorite vegetables. As a health-conscious weight watcher, I find a wedge of raw cabbage a fine substitute for forbidden food. It promotes well-being, assuages hunger, and lasts a long time, giving me a chance to marshal my will power when dieting.

In early spring, cabbage fills a vacuum until fresh local vegetables appear on the market and in the garden in abundance.

Raw cabbage blends successfully with all raw vegetables in salads. Here is a combination that grew from a standard coleslaw recipe because the other vegetables used were available during the winter in stores or from our freezer.

SUPERSLAW

½ medium cabbage	1 onion
1 large carrot	mayonnaise
¼ turnip	vinegar
2 or 3 Jerusalem artichokes	parsley, fresh dill fronds or
2 or 3 stalks celery	a few dill seeds, and caraway
1 green pepper	

Chop or shred the vegetables and combine them with mayonnaise, vinegar, and the seasonings (including salt and pepper). I use my own mayonnaise, which I make in a blender with garlic. The quantities of the seasonings are not rigid; they depend on what vegetables are available for use. Personally, I especially like some caraway seeds sprinkled in this coleslaw.

GARLIC MAYONNAISE

1 clove garlic, cut up	1 teaspoon dry mustard
1 egg	½ teaspoon salt
2 tablespoons vinegar or lemon juice	¼ teaspoon paprika
	1 cup olive or corn oil

Blend ¼ cup of the oil with the other ingredients for 1 minute. Lift cover of blender and add remainder of oil in a steady stream while blender is running. Shut off blender as soon as all oil is added.

The following Near Eastern cabbage dish was a favorite of mine when I was a little girl. I would nag my mother to make it often. I recently discovered that this cabbage and green pepper recipe can easily be converted into a delicious sweet-sour dish with the addition of 1 tablespoon honey or sugar and 1 to 2 tablespoons vinegar, depending on the tartness desired.

SPICED GREEN PEPPER AND CABBAGE

Churtma

3 tablespoons corn oil	½ cup water
1 onion, chopped	¼ teaspoon paprika
1 large green pepper, diced	2 tablespoons chopped fresh
small head cabbage, shredded	parsley (optional)
2 drops hot pepper sauce	few dill seeds
(optional)	½ teaspoon salt or more

Heat the oil in heavy large pot or skillet and sauté the onion, pepper, and cabbage for a few minutes. Add other ingredients, cover pot, and cook until vegetables are barely tender. Makes 4 generous servings.

Another versatile vegetable usually available throughout the winter is eggplant. Near Easterners have countless ways of cooking this vegetable, but it seems to be a novelty in some parts of the United States. I once had an eggplant in my shopping cart and two women stopped me to ask how I intended to cook it.

My grandmother taught me how to select a fresh eggplant if bought. The vegetable, she said, should have a deep purple unwrinkled skin with a bright green cap at the stem end. Eggplants with shriveled dry caps tend to be old and have a bitter taste. Some old-timers still salt eggplant slices, stack them, and set aside about 1 hour weighted with a heavy plate, to release the bitter juices. The slices are then washed, dried, and browned in oil before baking. I pass up this extra work and find my baked eggplant dishes are just as tasty. However, I am careful to use only fresh eggplant.

Here are three of our favorite recipes. I urge any of you who have never cooked eggplant to try one for a new experience in flavor. Everyone who has eaten eggplant at our house has gone overboard about this vegetable.

EGGPLANT STEW

1 eggplant	1 clove garlic, sliced
1 onion, slivered	2 cups canned tomatoes
3 tablespoons corn or olive oil	1 cup soup stock
1 green pepper, cut in small squares	salt and pepper

If the eggplant is fresh from the garden and tender, do not peel it. Cut it in 1-inch cubes, and set aside. Sauté the slivered onion in oil for 2 minutes, add the eggplant cubes and other ingredients, cover, and simmer until done. This stew is very good spooned over cooked rice or rice pilav. Makes 4 to 6 servings.

MEAT-STUFFED BAKED EGGPLANT

1 large eggplant, sliced	2 tablespoons chopped parsley
corn or olive oil	1 teaspoon chopped fresh dill fronds (optional)
1½ pounds ground lean lamb or beef	1 teaspoon chopped fresh basil (optional)
1 onion, chopped	
1 teaspoon curry powder	3 cups canned tomatoes or fresh sliced tomatoes
¼ cup pignolia or other nuts	
1 clove garlic, chopped	salt and pepper

In a heavy skillet, sauté the eggplant slices in oil, browning them lightly on both sides without cooking through. Keep adding oil as necessary, to prevent the slices from sticking to the skillet while browning. Set aside when done.

In the same skillet, combine meat, onion, nuts, garlic, spices, herbs, and seasoning with a tablespoon of oil. Sauté about 2 minutes, stirring once or twice.

Arrange a layer of the eggplant slices in the bottom of a large baking or roasting pan. Spread them with the meat mixture and cover with another layer of eggplant, dividing the slices evenly between the two layers. Pour the tomatoes over all or cover with thick slices of fresh tomatoes. Cover the pan with a sheet of foil and bake at 350° for about 30 minutes. Makes about 6 servings.

BAKED EGGPLANT AU GRATIN

2 to 4 tablespoons corn or olive
    oil
1 clove garlic, chopped
1 large onion, thinly sliced
1 large eggplant, sliced
salt and pepper

1 or 2 green peppers, sliced
3 cups canned tomatoes or fresh
    sliced tomatoes
shredded or sliced mild cheese
chopped parsley

Pour the oil in the bottom of a baking or roasting pan. Spread in
the onion slices and garlic, and top with 1/2-inch overlapping slices
of eggplant, then peppers. Season with salt and pepper and pour the
tomatoes over all or cover top with thick slices of fresh tomatoes.
Cover pan with foil and bake in 350° oven about 30 minutes. Remove
from oven, lift off foil, and cover top with the cheese, then sprinkle
with parsley. The cheese will melt by serving time. Makes about 6
servings.

I consider potatoes good cold weather fare also, and unjustly maligned in reducing diets. They are supposed to be fattening—but
many calorie charts show they are no more so than an apple, which
is approved diet food. What makes potatoes high-caloried is the butter or sour cream you add to them. Potatoes contain some vitamin C
and minerals too, especially when eaten with their skins.

Although the Irish sometimes get the credit, potatoes originated in
South America. The Spaniards found the Indians raising potatoes and
took some home to Spain; before very long the vegetable had become
popular throughout Europe and Ireland.

The Irish, who suffered through so much conflict and lost their
food supplies in raids, discovered that potatoes came out of the
ground unscathed. Later, it was a fungus-caused potato famine in
Ireland that sent many Irish to America—they were the first immi-
grants to plant large quantities of potatoes here.

The slang name of spud was coined in England when potatoes were
first introduced there. British wheat growers, fearing competition,
started rumors against the vegetable. They formed a league called the
Society for the Prevention of Unwholesome Diet, condensed to
"spud."

These recipes may give you a change from the usual methods of
serving spuds.

MEAT AND POTATO BAKE

8 potatoes	¼ teaspoon allspice
4 tablespoons butter	½ cup fresh chopped parsley *or*
1 pound ground beef	¼ cup dried parsley flakes
2 onions, chopped	1 egg, beaten
salt and pepper	

Cook the potatoes and mash them with the butter. Fry the meat for 5 minutes with the other ingredients (except the egg). Spread half the mashed potatoes in a buttered baking pan, top with the meat mixture and then the remaining potatoes. Cover with beaten egg, and bake in a 375° oven until the top browns. Cut in squares and serve. Makes 6 to 8 servings.

POTATO STEW

6 medium potatoes, sliced	2 tablespoons chopped parsley
1 cup canned tomatoes	1 clove garlic, minced
1 large carrot, sliced	4 tablespoons corn oil
2 stalks celery, chopped	2 cups meat stock or water

Combine all the ingredients in a large pot or skillet, cover, and simmer about 20 minutes. Makes 4 to 6 servings.

CONTINENTAL POTATO SALAD

3 cups sliced boiled potatoes	2 hard-boiled eggs, chopped
1 onion, chopped	chopped dill and parsley
2 stalks celery, chopped	1 cup plain yogurt or sour cream
1 green pepper, chopped	¼ teaspoon paprika
¼ cup sweet relish	salt and pepper

Combine all the ingredients, chill, and serve. I use flavor salt for seasoning. The amount of parsley or dill is a matter of taste. Both may be omitted if not available, or dried parsley or dillweed used. Makes 4 to 6 servings.

We generally restrict our consumption of sweets, and I use honey almost exclusively instead of sugar. One dismal spring day, I went down to the cellar to replenish my honey supply for the kitchen. I planned to make honey candy and other honey goodies for Jessica and Aram, my two grandchildren in Florida.

Usually I buy honey in quantity from Ozzie, our neighbor at Hillside Orchards. Ozzie and his family live up the road from us, and his farm nestles against a high hill. He keeps bees to pollinate his acres of apple and pear orchards and his raspberry, blueberry, and strawberry patches. The bees come here first in the spring, as our plum trees blossom before Ozzie's trees.

Years ago when I had a chance to buy a couple of beehives at a bargain price, George protested, claiming he was not about to play nursemaid to a bunch of bees in his old age. He remained adamant against all my arguments in favor of hives on the farm. Finally I gave up and talked Ozzie into buying the hives. Since then, he has added many more hives, and now we all benefit.

Honey deserves wider use in the home for both health and appetite appeal. It gives a distinctive flavor to puddings, custards, baked apples, candied vegetables, and many other foods when substituted for sugar. It contains small amounts of minerals, protein, and vitamins, too.

Honey was used in baked foods as a preservative long before chemicals were discovered to be cheaper and handier. Nearly all pastries and breads made with honey have superior keeping qualities. Cakes and cookies stay moist in storage when some honey is used for part of the sugar. In some instances, their texture and flavor even improves when they are aged a few days.

During the Middle Ages, honey was used plain or mixed with other ingredients for wounds, burns, and ulcers. It was the first antiseptic. Experiments have shown that most bacteria cannot live in honey.

In baked products, better results are obtained with honey if some baking soda in addition to baking powder is used, since honey needs an alkali like soda. According to a U.S. Department of Agriculture bulletin, in experiments it was found that the allowance of soda to 1 cup of honey ranged between ¼ and half teaspoon, varying with the type of honey. Honey can be substituted for up to half the sugar in a recipe without changing any other ingredients.

HONEY CAKE

3 or 4 eggs	1 teaspoon baking soda
1 cup sugar	1 teaspoon salt
1 cup honey	1 cup hot milk
2 cups flour	4 tablespoons corn oil
2 teaspoons baking powder	1 teaspoon vanilla

Beat the eggs with the sugar until very light, about 5 minutes. While beating, add the honey in a thin stream. Combine the flour, baking powder, soda, and salt and fold into the egg mixture. Add the milk, oil, and vanilla and again fold in. Bake in an 8 x 12 inch pan at 350° about 40 minutes. For an upsidedown cake, cover the bottom of the pan with fresh fruit or berries, sweetened with honey or sugar, or drained sweetened canned fruit.

I substitute a mixture of 1 tablespoon soya powder and 4 tablespoons of raw wheat germ for the same amount of the flour, and add 1 heaping tablespoon powdered milk to the dry ingredients. This cake is easy to make and improves with storage.

NUTTY HONEY JUMBLES

1 cup honey	1 tablespoon boiling water
2 tablespoons corn oil	2 cups flour
¾ teaspoon baking soda	¼ to ½ cup chopped nuts
½ teaspoon salt	

Combine the honey and oil in a mixing bowl. In a teacup, combine the soda, salt, and boiling water, and add this to the honey mixture. Blend in the flour and fold in the chopped nuts. Refrigerate the dough a few hours before rolling it out and cutting it into shapes. Bake about 12 minutes in a 350° oven. This is a delicately flavored, crisp cookie, fine for children. Makes about 2½ dozen cookies.

NUTTY HONEY CANDY

This unusual candy is in a class by itself. I cannot take credit for inventing it, but can vouch for its delicious flavor and superior quality. It improves with age and will keep indefinitely without becoming sticky. The more nuts used, the better it will taste.

3 cups honey	1 tablespoon butter
½ cup tart apple pulp	1 cup or more chopped nuts

Combine the honey and apple pulp in a large saucepan and boil rapidly to the firm ball stage, about 254° on a candy thermometer. Toward the end, keep stirring to prevent burning. Add butter and chopped nuts and pour into an 8 x 12 inch buttered pan. Cut in squares before the candy is entirely cold.

HONEY BREAD PUDDING

8 slices bread	¼ teaspoon allspice
½ cup raisins	1 tablespoon cinnamon
3 cups hot milk	¼ teaspoon nutmeg
½ cup honey	2 eggs, beaten

Cut the bread slices each into four pieces and arrange them in a baking pan. Sprinkle with raisins that have been plumped in hot water. Combine the milk, honey, and spices, and gradually add to the beaten eggs. Pour the mixture over the bread squares, and bake at 350° for 30 to 45 minutes, until puffy and crusty. I use my whole wheat bread and also add ¼ cup powdered milk to the liquid milk for added nutrition. Makes 6 to 8 servings.

To compensate for the prolonged raw, chilly weather, I made fried cheese turnovers one day for lunch. I recommend these to all cheese lovers as a fast, cheesy hot treat.

FRIED CHEESE TURNOVERS

1 egg, beaten	2 cups flour
2 tablespoons corn oil	1 teaspoon baking powder
1 tablespoon honey or sugar	½ teaspoon salt
½ cup milk	¼ cup powdered milk (optional)

Beat together the liquid ingredients. Combine the dry ingredients, and stir the two mixtures together to make a medium dough. Add more milk if it is too stiff or more flour if too loose. Knead a minute or two, cover with a damp cloth, and set aside while making the cheese filling, which is the same as the one for cheese boats (see index).

Roll out pieces of dough to the size of a dessert plate, about ⅛ inch thick. Spread the filling on one half of each round, leaving the edges free. Moisten the edges, fold the other half of the dough over the filling, and seal the edges with the tines of a fork.

Fry in hot oil until slightly browned, turning once. My chatty directions may give the impression that this recipe is a lot of work but it really isn't. Anyhow, I feel creative cooking for proper nutrition is rewarding activity.

To perk up early spring dishes, here is a really super condiment that the Japanese call gomasio and I call sesame salt. It was first served to me by a friend who also believes in pure foods and creative cooking. She told me how to make it.

SESAME SALT

Combine 1 part salt to 8 parts sesame seeds, preferably with hulls, in a heavy skillet. Stir and roast over medium heat for about 10 minutes. Grind coarsely in a blender or a suribachi, which is a type of glorified mortar with a wooden pestle. Although the blender is faster and easier, I bought a suribachi as the blender was aesthetically unsatisfactory to me.

Now I use the suribachi to combine my own blend of flavor salt, too. I decided to make my own when I discovered that the commercial variety contained preservatives. Why preservatives should be necessary in such a mixture I can't imagine.

Since I began making my own, I vacillate between using sesame salt and flavor salt on cooked vegetables and meat and egg dishes.

FLAVOR SALT

8 tablespoons salt	½ teaspoon oregano
1 tablespoon curry powder	½ teaspoon tarragon
1 tablespoon dried parsley	½ teaspoon dried celery leaves
1 teaspoon garlic powder	1 teaspoon dried basil

Combine ½ the salt with the other spices and herbs in the suribachi; then blend in the remaining salt; or crush dry herbs with salt and stir in the curry and garlic powders.

Other spices may be used and quantities varied according to preference. My curry powder is an Indian brand, so it may be stronger than the domestic mixtures. It is certainly hotter.

While I am still in the doldrums waiting for a warm sunny spell, let me show you how to make yogurt at home for a fraction of the cost of store-bought yogurt. It is as common as milk in homes where ancestors came from Near Eastern countries, and very easy to make.

Yogurt, called *matzoon* by Armenians, was our children's first solid food and they thrived on it. They have always eaten it in one form or another and still like it.

Yogurt is another versatile food; it can be used in the same manner as sour cream in many recipes. Mix it with cottage cheese and honey for a fruit salad dressing. As a dessert, try some with honey or maple syrup drizzled on top, or a dollop of jam in the center.

TO MAKE YOGURT

Heat 1 or 2 quarts of milk in a heavy utensil over medium heat to the boiling point, being careful it does not boil over. I use whole milk, which forms a skin on top. Holding the skin back, pour the milk into an earthenware container with cover, slipping the skin on the top surface. My mother had a special yogurt bowl with cover, but I use one utensil for both operations, the kind that withstands both high heat and severe cold. A small bean pot with cover should do if no other bowl is available.

Cool the milk, uncovered, until slightly warmer than lukewarm. Use ¼ to ½ cup of plain commercial yogurt, not Swiss-style (it won't work), for starter. Stir a little of the warm milk in the starter, then pour the starter mixture into the crock of warm milk, under the skin, stirring it a little. Cover and set the crock in a warm place for about 8 hours until the milk becomes the consistency of custard.

The old-timers covered the crock with one or two Turkish towels and left it on the counter. I warm my oven and set the yogurt container in it, putting the oven on again when it cools, if I think of it. The yogurt usually "takes" anyway even if I forget. Once, I completely forgot the yogurt and it stayed in the oven two days, but it was fine when we ate it. After you make your own yogurt, be sure to save some as starter for the next batch.

When we first moved up here, yogurt was not readily available in stores. I was making some one day for the children and had left my starter in a small bowl on the kitchen counter as I busied myself elsewhere while the milk cooled. When I returned to the kitchen to make the yogurt, I discovered our cat had jumped up and eaten the starter. I used the milk for something else, and waited for my mother to visit and bring me fresh starter.

The old-time yogurt was never flavored as yogurt is today in food stores. The plain variety was necessary for the many ways this fine food was used, especially in cooked recipes.

Yogurt, thinned and beaten with a little water, makes a refreshing drink similar to buttermilk, especially in the summer.

Here is a dandy gourmet yogurt recipe I just remembered. My mother made it when I was a child and I have never seen it anywhere.

I used to make it years ago for lunch. My mother, who may have invented the dish, used thin Armenian cracker bread, broken into small pieces, as the base but I don't see why crisp unbuttered toast or croutons cannot be used. Now, what shall I call it? How about

HOT YOGURT SURPRISE

toasted bread squares or croutons	2 large sliced onions
1 egg	¼ cup butter
1 pint plain yogurt	¼ teaspoon salt

Cover the bottom of two large soup plates with the toasted bread or croutons. In the top of a double boiler, beat the egg and yogurt together and heat over boiling water, adding the salt. The egg prevents the yogurt from curdling.

Fry the onions in the butter until tender. Spoon half the hot yogurt over toast in each dish and cover the yogurt with the butter and onion mixture. Stir and add more salt if needed. Makes 2 generous servings.

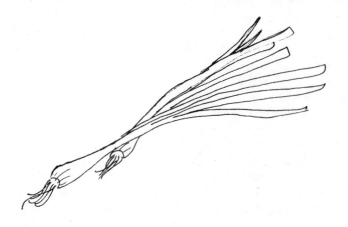

May

HE LAST patch of snow has finally disappeared and the days have lengthened. We pushed back the mulch in the garden to expose the rows of soil to the warm sun.

I try to get most of the garden planted before the blackflies come out and harass me. Planting is strictly my job—it has been during all the years we have had a garden. George helps later with the little weeding we do between the seedlings in the rows. I usually identify the vegetable seedlings first, since one year he pulled out the vegetables and left the weeds.

When the ground dries out enough, I'm ready to plant without having to wait for a neighboring farmer to get around to plowing up the plot, as we had to do before we went "organic" with mulch. I find a long-handled cultivator or potato digger easiest to work with when pushing the mulch aside for row crops and loosening the soil for planting.

I remember my frustration in the past, as I plotted devious ways to nag the farmer to get to our garden so that I wouldn't be the last one in the area to plant, as usually happened. Now, all I do after pushing aside the mulch is put in the seeds, beginning with the peas, as soon as the ground can be worked.

I try to rotate my crops, especially the peas, which do not produce well unless moved each year. Along with tomatoes, corn, cabbage, broccoli, and cauliflower, they are heavy feeders. Rotating crops also prevents certain plant diseases, such as clubfoot and cabbage worm in the cabbage family. Parsley, broccoli, chard, carrots, radishes, and other hardy seeds are planted at the same time as the peas. I plant corn, zucchini, cucumber, melon, and winter squash seeds about the middle of May in our area, central New Hampshire.

Around Memorial Day at the end of May, the seedlings and plants on the porch are transferred to the garden. Sometimes I take a chance and put out a few earlier and cover them during frost-warning periods. But I find that plants put out later when the ground is warmer often catch up with the ones planted earlier. As usual, rather than bother with collars around the plants to prevent cutworm destruction, I sprinkle wood ashes around each. Since I heard about this method of cutworm control three years ago, practiced by an old farmer and now me, I have never lost a plant and it takes me half as long to set them out. During the blackfly season, every minute counts.

After all the planting is done, we replenish the mulch by adding more hay or leaves, since the bottom layer disintegrates and composts into the soil. Weeding is practically eliminated by this method. Every three or four years, we also spread rotted cow manure, available from a neighbor's farm, over the garden in the fall before mulching with hay or leaves. I don't know whether the garden needs it or not, but figure we should play it safe.

Since we started burying our garbage deep in the garden—in the snow during the winter to be turned under in the spring—my hybrid worms have multiplied and the garden soil is black and rich. The worms, as I explained earlier, were one of my many get-rich-quick ventures that fizzled. Although I did not get rich, I became an expert on worm culture—for what that's worth. Finally, I decided to give up selling worms to fishermen and use them instead to enrich our garden and small fruit orchard. We buried worms under every fruit tree we planted.

I must say George has been very tolerant through the years about my various loony projects to help strengthen our weak financial position. Someday they may all be compiled for posterity under the unique title *Ten Projects to Make Money on the Farm That Failed*—to make money, that is. I sure became an expert in many areas, knowledge I probably will never use again. Back to the garden:

Several years ago, I spaded up a small plot next to the vegetable garden for herbs. We have had a running battle with it ever since. I combined a clump of chives, some spearmint, and perennial onions in the herb garden the first year, and let it go at that, since these herbs were all perennials. Gradually the onions and spearmint took over, so one spring George dug most of them out and I planted sage, savory, marjoram, and basil, the herbs I use most. The sage and basil survived, but the spearmint and onions crawled into the savory and marjoram and killed them.

Recently, when I was given a comfrey plant, I had the good sense to ask if and how it multiplied. When I heard, I planted it in back of the rhubarb bed! Comfrey is supposed to be good for everything that ails you. According to the herb chapter in my 1910 copy of the *People's Home Medical Book*, which I found at a rummage sale (where else does one acquire such gems?), a "decoction" made with comfrey root and water is good for internal injuries, erosions of the bowels, coughs, and "female weaknesses."

Seriously, though, the healing drug in comfrey is allantoin, and no home should be without it, we are told. According to one source, eighteenth-century herbalists considered comfrey an infallible remedy for external and internal wounds, bruises, ruptures, and stomach ulcers.

Here, too, I can cite Euell Gibbons. In *Stalking the Healthful Herbs*, he says that the first leaves of the plant, gathered in March or April, make a delicious dish of greens "equal to spinach and better than chard." I got my plant too late to try it but shall do so next spring.

Gibbons claims that if *he* had stomach ulcers, he would follow his physician's instructions but would make sure his diet also included large amounts of comfrey. How would it be available if ulcers developed in the winter? One freezes the tender greens in the spring, of course.

My method of using herbs is to experiment with quantities of flavors. Herb and spice charts give basic information on the foods with which each herb is compatible. Herbs should be used to enhance, not overpower. One-fourth teaspoon in a recipe for four persons is considered the right amount for a dried herb. Three or four times that amount of fresh herbs can be used.

Herbs can easily be dried. One method is to tie them up in bunches after cutting and hang them in the sun in crisp, cold weather. Or pick off the leaves, spread them in trays, and dry on radiators or in a slow oven, after which they can be crumbled and stored in airtight containers.

We organic gardeners are also using herbs to fight unwelcome insects in the vegetable garden, as a method of biological control against pollution. For instance, garlic and chives help control aphids. Mustard helps keep cabbage insect pests away. Summer savory is supposed to repel the Mexican beetle, and basil planted in the tomato patch is supposed to protect the plants. I cannot vouch for all these methods, as we have seldom found harmful insects in our garden since we went organic.

At this time of year on the farm, we fall asleep to the sound of peepers and awake to the tranquil songs of birds, a far cry from the cacophony of city noise. In spite of my apprehension about winter driving, I feel my permanent home will remain in the Northeast, where the changing seasons each contribute to the beauty of nature.

Our fruit orchard is in various stages of bloom, the lawns are a rich green, and blue forget-me-nots are in flower in the perennial border by the swale stone wall. I began perfuming the house with fresh flowers—trillium from the woods and lilac from our huge bush by the corner field.

Edible greens and nature bouquets to fill both my physical and my aesthetic needs are at their best in May, when the bright sun has melted away all memory of snow. In my periodic forages in search of them in fields and woods, I take a Boy Scout knife left by one of my sons. It is a sturdy instrument and can be carried closed for safety. I have long since replaced the lovely baskets of yesteryear with the modern lightweight plastic pails as being more practical.

I must be a charming sight swinging down the road, sometimes with field glasses around my neck for bird watching, dressed in old blue jeans and shirt. The pièce de résistance, of course, is a straw hat with high crown on which a stuffed owl perches contemplating a couple of artificial flying bees. It is sometimes changed for another favorite straw hat, white with a wide brim, the front pinned back with a huge artificial red rose.

Would that I were more informed on edible greens—I'm sure I'm missing out on many growing around our farm.

I limit my spring pickings to dandelions, milkweed shoots, and young stinging nettles. Those of you who have come in contact with stinging nettles during the summer will find this hard to believe, but when they are picked in early spring (wear gloves!), nettles cooked like other greens make a tasty dish to set before anyone. According to my nature guru Euell Gibbons in *Stalking the Healthful Herbs*, this weed is extremely rich in vitamins A and C and "very efficacious in reducing corpulency," probably why I tried it in the first place.

Gibbons gives several recipes for cooking nettles and extols the virtues of nettle juice. I can vouch for both although I did not reduce "corpulency." Before reading his book, my only experience with nettles was to try to recognize the plant mixed in with wild raspberries in an old cellar hole when I went picking. Many was the time, in my excitement to pick the loaded bushes, that I brushed against the horrible weed and suffered the consequences. Since we now have our own raspberries, I go to the cellar hole to pick the nettles.

BUTTERED NETTLES

Wash the nettles and steam them for 20 minutes in just the water that adheres to them. (Cooking destroys the nettles' stinging properties.) Drain, season with salt and pepper, and serve with butter.

Gibbons says that in the olden days this weed was used for medicinal purposes and as an antidote for poisoning by hemlock and nightshade. It was also used to cure scurvy and other vitamin C deficiencies. The pot liquor is delicious, seasoned with salt, pepper, and a little vinegar, to drink hot or cold.

I learned how tasty milkweed spears were after Babe and Dave ate some at a neighboring farmer's home. We had then only recently moved into the country from the city. The boys, about eight and ten years old at the time, were picky eaters who were not especially fond of vegetables. When they returned home that day raving about the delicious milkweed sprouts served to them, I decided this free vegetable deserved further investigation. They were right.

BUTTERED MILKWEED SPEARS

Pick the spears before the leaves unfurl and wash them. Steam in a little water until tender. Season with salt and pepper, add butter, and serve. They may be creamed or served with hollandaise sauce, too.

I arose early on a glorious Saturday to the songs of birds welcoming the beautiful day. While having coffee on the porch, I watched a downy woodpecker peck at the suet still hanging from the yellow plum tree, ready to burst into bloom (the tree, that is).

After breakfast, I decided to check out the dandelions in our corner field. With the field glasses around my neck for bird watching on the side, I grabbed my Scout knife and plastic pail and started down the road, lustily singing Mana-Zucca's "I Love Life!" and meaning every word of it. Luckily, we have no close neighbors.

The dandelions were perfect for picking, full grown between clumps of grass for easy digging, the buds still tight buttons in the centers. It was a cool windy morning; the blackflies must have been sleeping because they weren't around. I made two trips to the field, returning each time with the 10-quart pail tightly packed with greens. Using the water in the rain barrel, I washed them, then boiled them for 3 minutes in water to cover, to eliminate the bitterness. I froze 7 quart packages for later consumption. Frozen dandelion cooks in about 10 minutes and fresh dandelion cooks in about 15 minutes.

The lowly dandelion is an excellent source of calcium, potassium, and vitamin A. Although some of the vitamins may be lost by cooking in water to cover, I feel in this case the method is justified to make the greens palatable. After cooking, they may be buttered, seasoned, and served, or here is another dandy way to serve them.

DANDELIONS WITH ONIONS

Wash and cut up dandelion greens, and cook them in water to cover. Drain well, pressing against colander or strainer, and put aside. In a large skillet, sauté a slivered large onion in a mixture of 2 to 4 tablespoons of corn oil and butter mixed. When the onions are soft, add the greens, season with salt and pepper, stir, heat through and serve. Use about a quart of drained greens.

Sometimes I add a handful of fresh-roasted shelled peanuts to sauté with the onions just before they are cooked. This gives the dish a gourmet touch and impresses guests.

Just as I finished freezing the dandelions, a friend I had invited bottle digging arrived, so we spent the rest of the morning and part of the afternoon tramping through the woods to several dumps I knew of. Other diggers had cleaned them out. Although we found no bottles, I thoroughly enjoyed my walk in the woods, returning with one trillium to grace the porch bouquet of wild cherry blossoms.

DANDELION WINE

Several days later, I noticed yellow dandelion flowers dotting the corner field where I had picked the greens. Never one to waste anything, I decided to make wine, and collected 2 gallons of blooms. I put the blossoms in a large crock, covered them with 2 gallons of boiling water, and pushed the crock (with its cover on) under the kitchen table. After three days, George strained the mixture through several layers of cheesecloth, ready for me to carry out the next step of converting the liquid into wine.

I discovered why it would have been wiser to make one batch instead of doubling it. I had no cauldron large enough for the next step, so—judging by look—I divided the liquid into two pots. To each pot, I added the thinly pared peel and the juice of one orange and one lemon and 3 pounds of sugar.

After boiling it gently for about 30 minutes, I poured the mixture from both pots back into the crock. Next step was softening one package of dry yeast in a little warm water and spreading it over a slice of toast. When the contents of the crock had cooled to luke-warm, I floated the toast on top of the liquid. This time I covered the crock with a cloth.

Six days later, we strained the wine into gallon jugs, corked them lightly with wadded cotton, and stuck the jugs in a dark corner in the cellar for three weeks, after which George decanted the wine into bottles, corking them tightly for storage until Christmas. Then we can get our feet wet and have an excuse to imbibe!

I usually suggest corking instead of screw tops because a glass jug kept on working and blew up one year. It made a worse mess than the day years ago when Babe pulled the bung out of the cider barrel after the cider had started to ferment. Then, fortunately, I was standing by with a pot, waiting to siphon out some cider. For a moment, overcome with amazement, we watched the geyser spurt out of the barrel all over the cellar. Finally, I woke up and handed the pot to Babe, who held it under the cider while I ran upstairs for a pail. At the end of that scene, we were both bathed in cider.

The next weekend gave us a chance to finish planting the garden and catch up with other outside work.

The rhubarb patch, with tiny stalks the last time I looked, was in full growth, tall and lush, hiding the ground underneath. We almost lost the plants last year and, through the mishap, met a new neighbor. Actually, we met his young bull first—or maybe it was a heifer. I was more frightened because I didn't know.

It was early spring, and George was fiddling in the rhubarb patch when suddenly the animal stood behind him, having emerged from our woodsy swale. I alerted George and said "Shoo!" to the visitor, but the dumb animal stood there and glared at me.

Besides being scared, I was frantic at the thought that it might trample our other garden, too. While George grabbed a nearby rake and tried to ward off the bull and head it toward the road, I dashed into the house and began calling neighbors to ask if anyone in the vicinity was missing a bull or cow. One person told me it probably belonged to new neighbors down the road a piece. When I couldn't find them listed in the phone book, I stumbled into my car and drove down.

A man and several children were tending various animals milling around outside the place. Without taking time to introduce myself, I demanded, "Is that bull or cow in our yard yours?" He thought it was. "Will you please remove it immediately!" He and the children were climbing into his station wagon almost before I finished.

I got my car out of the way, then fell in behind him, wondering if he knew where we lived. He did.

George was jousting with the bull in front of our barn when we got there, the animal having toured the area acreage during my absence, I later learned. They were both in a state of acute distress when the neighbor and his children took over and corralled the critter. Led by the animal on a rope, they all disappeared down the road.

George dropped the rake and sat down by the picnic table and started fanning himself. I joined him because I was steaming, too, but for other reasons. I remembered hearing that animals had escaped before from that farm, raising havoc in other gardens. Farmers way back had told us there was a law against that. It was considered the cardinal sin.

George ran true to form with, "Don't you think I should go down and give him a lift back so he can get his car?"

"It would serve him right to walk, but go ahead," I said. What's the use?

When they came back, I explained that we were too old to chase anything, least of all bulls, and would he please see that the animals were penned more securely in the future? He apologized for the bull's intrusion. After that, we had a friendly visit, and now we wave to each other when we pass on the road.

OLD-FASHIONED RHUBARB SHORTCAKE

4 cups cut rhubarb	½ cup milk (about)
cinnamon and nutmeg	2 tablespoons sugar or honey
1 cup sugar (about)	1½ cups flour
1 egg	1 tablespoon baking powder
4 tablespoons corn oil	½ teaspoon salt

Line an 8 x 12 inch pan with rhubarb cut into 1-inch pieces. (Do not peel.) Shake spices over the rhubarb and sprinkle with 1 cup or more of sugar, depending on the sweetness desired.

In a bowl, beat the egg with the oil, milk, and the 2 tablespoons of sugar (or honey). Combine the dry ingredients in another bowl. Stir the liquid mixture into the dry ingredients, adding more milk, if necessary, for a sloppy dough, almost a thick batter. Spread this over the rhubarb mixture, and bake about 20 minutes at 400°. (I add a heaping tablespoon of powdered milk to the dry ingredients, and use part stone-ground whole wheat flour.)

CRUNCHY RHUBARB PUDDING

4 cups cut rhubarb	1 teaspoon baking powder
cinnamon and nutmeg	⅛ teaspoon salt
1 cup sugar, about	¼ cup sugar
1 cup flour	1 egg, beaten

Again, line an 8 x 12 inch pan with rhubarb cut in 1-inch pieces. Shake spices over the rhubarb and sprinkle with 1 cup or more sugar, depending on the sweetness desired.

Combine all other ingredients in a bowl for a mealy, crumbly mixture. Sprinkle this over the rhubarb and bake about 20 minutes in a 400° oven. Embellish with whipped cream or ice cream if desired. (I use stone-ground whole wheat flour.)

RHUBARB BREAD PUDDING

8 slices toasted bread
1½ cups hot milk
4 tablespoons corn oil
3 eggs, slightly beaten
1 cup honey or sugar

1 teaspoon cinnamon
¼ teaspoon salt
2 cups cut rhubarb
½ cup wheat germ (optional)

Line an 8 x 12 inch pan with toast cut in squares. Add milk and oil and let set about 10 minutes. Combine and stir in the eggs, honey or sugar, cinnamon, salt, and rhubarb. Sprinkle with wheat germ, if used, and bake in 350° over about 45 minutes.

After making the dandelion wine, I decided to make rhubarb wine too, and revive this form of creative art.

I abandoned winemaking when our family dwindled to two after the boys moved to homes of their own and Gail went to college. When I started years ago, though, I learned a few things about winemaking the hard way and ended up a fairly good winemaker, judging by the compliments I received. The first thing I learned was not to do too much wine tasting at one time, as my tolerance for alcoholic beverages is extremely low. I also learned, as already mentioned, to use corks instead of screw tops on bottles containing wine still fermenting.

My first blackberry wine was delicious when I bottled it, but began turning into wine vinegar soon afterward, probably because I left the screw top loose for fear fermenting had not stopped. Later, when I got smart and used corks, I lost a few corks instead of both wine and bottles. My advice to home winemakers is to check corked bottles periodically and keep extra corks on hand, especially if the wine is stored in the cellar.

After I got the hang of winemaking, our wine cellar included some really good parsley, citrus fruit, elderberry, potato, raisin, and rhubarb wines.

Making wine for home use is easy, fun, and within the law. According to a general information bulletin on homemade wines published by the Educational Research Bureau in Washington, D.C., two hundred gallons of wine for the use of one's own family may be made annually at home without payment of revenue tax if none is sold or removed from the premises. The exemption will not apply if wines are made by one person for the use of another, or to wines produced by a single person unless he is the head of a family, or to wines produced by a married man living apart from his family, or to wines furnished to ranch hands or boarders. According to the bulletin, each person entitled to and desiring to avail himself of the exemption must file a notice with the collector of internal revenue before beginning to manufacture wine.

Now that that's out of the way, the next thing to do is find a crock or clean keg. Small casks that are sour may be cleaned by putting in a couple of ounces of unslaked lime, whatever that is, and filling with water, the bulletin states. The keg should be shaken if possible and then rolled over and over. Dump out and rinse with clear water, boiling water if available. Mustiness can be removed by burning a little sulfur in the empty casks. Bung, and let stand for a day.

RHUBARB WINE

Cut the rhubarb in pieces and put them in an enamel pot. Cover with water and simmer for 45 minutes. Strain through cheesecloth, measure juice, and add 3 pounds of sugar to each gallon of juice after pouring into a large crock. Cool to lukewarm.

Soften one package dry yeast in a little warm water, spread over a slice of toast, and float the toast on the liquid. Cover the crock with a cloth to keep out the insects, and set in a warm place to ferment for about 2 weeks. After the fermenting period, strain the liquid into gallon jugs and cork with wadded cotton. Store the jugs in a dark area for 3 weeks.

At the end of 3 weeks—handling the jugs gently to keep from disturbing the silt at the bottom—siphon or decant the contents into bottles, corking them tightly. (We save fancy liquor bottles, collecting most from friends and relatives.) Store until Christmas, when you should have delicious, clear rhubarb wine. You will have to taste this wine to believe how good it is.

BLACKBERRY WINE

Figuring 1 quart of syrup for each quart of berries, boil 1 gallon of water with 3 pounds of sugar to the thin syrup stage.

Mash 4 quarts of berries. Add an equal amount of boiling syrup, ½ pound raisins, and 1 package dry yeast when lukewarm. Cover with cloth and let stand in a warm place for 7 days.

Skim off the top scum and strain the liquid through several layers of cheesecloth. Cover and let stand until fermenting stops, about 3 or 4 days. Skim off the top again. Ladle into bottles, cork, and store in a cool place for several weeks.

To make blackberry brandy, add 1 pint of brandy to each gallon of juice.

ELDERBERRY WINE

Using only enough water to keep the berries from burning, simmer them for about 15 minutes. Strain through cheesecloth and add 8 cups of sugar to 10 cups of berry juice. When the juice is lukewarm, float a piece of toast smeared with one package of softened yeast on top, and set in a warm place to ferment. Skim daily. Strain, bottle, and cork when fermenting stops.

WILD GRAPE WINE

Use 1½ pounds of sugar to each 4 pounds of grapes. Put the grapes in a crock. Dissolve the sugar in 2 quarts of boiling water. Cool to lukewarm, then add one package of dry yeast and pour the mixture over the grapes in the crock. Cover the crock with cloth and set it in a warm place. When the mixture stops fermenting, press it through a strainer, bottle, and cork. Bottle in gallon jugs and decant or siphon into smaller bottles without disturbing silt at the bottom.

RAISIN BRANDY

This recipe, given to me by a German friend, makes a very potent brandy. It's one of the best homemade remedies for what ails you, pleasant to take and easy to make.

Dissolve 3 pounds brown sugar in 1 gallon boiling water in a crock. Cool; then add 2 pounds raisins and 1 pound whole-grain wheat, and stir. While mixture is still lukewarm, add 2 packages dry yeast and 2 egg whites. Cover the crock with a cloth and let it stand in a warm place, stirring well 1 minute each day for 14 days.

Strain through double cheesecloth into gallon jugs, and plug these with cotton until fermenting stops. Then cork tightly and store for several months until the brandy is clear. Siphon or decant it into smaller bottles and cork tightly.

We slide our wine crocks under the kitchen table. If the mixtures need stirring or skimming, the fermenting fruity odor reminds us to attend to the task. Besides, a tantalizingly different aroma permeates our farm kitchen.

I was in the garden planting corn and chuckling to myself when George went by and heard me.

"You cracking up?" he asked.

"Funny, aren't you! I was thinking of the day when we put in our first garden and the minister came to call while I was planting potatoes."

"He must have figured you dropped out of *Tobacco Road*," George commented as he walked away to whatever he was piddling with at the moment.

We were green new arrivals in the area at that time and had been told that it was a good thing to put plants and seeds in the ground before a rain. For some reason, we had decided to plant a large patch of potatoes although we were not heavy potato eaters. The seed potatoes were cut up and ready for planting when the day dawned wet and rainy. I decided to plant them anyway, figuring it would take more than rain to melt me, and I invited Babe and Dave to get into old clothes and help. After donning a torn pair of dungarees, an old sweatshirt belonging to George, and an old straw hat we'd found in the barn, to keep the rain out of my face, I was in a quandary over what to wear on my feet. The garden had been freshly plowed and harrowed and the rain was turning it into a sea of mud. Then I spotted an old pair of George's shoes and concluded they'd be just the thing.

The garden was to be in our corner field within sight of the house. Just as we finished and started back down the road, we noticed a car pulling into our driveway. Hurrying back the rest of the distance, we discovered the visitor was the minister of the village church. He had come to welcome us and invite us to attend services.

I stammered an explanation as I stood before him, feeling like a fat scarecrow. If the minister was shocked by our appearance, he didn't show it. The boys scooted off, and I excused myself to clean up, then served tea. We had a lovely visit, and five years later he christened baby Gail before he retired.

June

I WAS WALKING through the back pasture to check out the Mayflowers, which were late this year, when I remembered the day I outfoxed Hazen, our ornery ram, more than 20 years ago. It happened in late fall, when the boys were in school, George at work, and I was home alone. I had been freezing corn and decided to feed the husks to the pigs. In those days we were trying to be as self-sufficient as possible, so we had a variety of animals on the farm. The two pigs had a small house and pen in the sheep pasture.

I went to the pasture gate with the bushel basket of husks and paused to check Hazen's position. He was at the far end of the pasture, grazing with his back to me. I calculated I could make it to the pen and back without attracting his attention.

Silently I unlatched the gate and went to the pen, but I hadn't figured on the reaction of Cynthia and Christopher, our pigs. They greeted me with happy oinks, causing Hazen to raise his huge head to see what was going on.

When he spotted me, he lowered his head and charged. I should explain here that my running ability was considerably hampered at that time by the fact that I was expecting Gail. I knew I couldn't beat Hazen to the gate—so, thinking fast, I stood my ground and waited. As he reached me, I stepped aside like a bull fighter, only my cape was the basket, which I draped over his head. By the time he shook it off, I had enough of a head start to make it to the gate.

We bought Hazen when he was a lamb, and he grew into a beautiful huge animal; we used him for breeding our flock. The first time I had tangled with him was the year before. I bent over one day to grain the lambs and he butted me, sending me almost through the tie-up wall! We all kept our distance after that, but he caught the boys off guard on rare occasions, once treeing Dave. Babe heard Dave's cries and rescued him by attracting Hazen's attention. While the ram chased Babe, Dave climbed down and got away.

Well, I found no Mayflowers but plenty of blackflies. They can really make a beautiful day miserable.

HERB LORE

I froze several small bunches of ferny dill from the clumps that still come up annually through natural reseeding. Only after inserting the ferny tops into small plastic bags, and closing the bags with rubber bands, do I cut off the protruding stems. Once the dill is frozen, I shall store all the plastic bags together in a labeled paper bag for easy identification. In the winter, the dill is wonderful for coleslaw and to enhance potato and other salads.

As soon as the parsley, a biennial, comes up from the previous year, and the scallions, which are planted early, I chop and combine them with chopped green peppers, put the mixture in a plastic container, and store it in the refrigerator for general use. These greens can be sprinkled on all sorts of foods—soups, cooked vegetables, and shish-kebab, especially when served in split homemade Armenian or Syrian flatbread.

I usually dry parsley, but last year froze some, bunching small "bouquets" of the leaf portion tied together and leaving short stems. Without steaming or any other treatment, I froze the bunches on a tray, then bagged them in plastic. It wasn't as good as fresh parsley but better than the dried form in some recipes.

I've taken to chewing parsley these days for two reasons—because this herb is extremely nutritious and to mask my passion for garlic, even in the flavor salt I sprinkle on my breakfast eggs. I began to suspect I was guilty of offending when several persons gently backed off as I was talking to them.

Parsley is a favorite herb, and I use it frequently in foods. It is rich in vitamins and minerals. Recently I learned it also acts as a diuretic. It was used for medicinal purposes in the early days to cleanse the blood and to correct kidney and bladder disorders and flatulence. During World War I, many English soldiers who were victims of certain kidney disorders associated with dysentery were cured by drinking parsley tea.

This is made by steeping 1 heaping teaspoonful of dried parsley leaves in 1 cup of hot water until the water gets cold. Strain and heat. Or a heaping tablespoon of leaves may be simmered in a quart of hot water for 30 minutes, then strained and served. I have never tried the tea, but may do so this winter. In the meantime, I'll just chew on fresh parsley. Hopefully, it will curb my eating, too.

My goodness! I just discovered that parsley is good for female troubles, urinary troubles, dropsy, vermin, bruises, bites, and stings, according to my copy of the *People's Home Medical Book*. The book says to use the fresh root for tea, using one ounce of root to a pint of water, taken hot. Fomentations of the leaves are applied for bites and insect stings. "The seeds and leaves sprinkled on the hair will destroy vermin," the book promises.

Here are two delicious parsley dinner recipes, which I serve with garlic bread and sweet corn.

PARSLEY EGG SALAD

3 or 4 hard-boiled eggs	¼ cup chopped dill fronds
1 cup chopped parsley	(optional)
1 small green pepper, chopped	salt and pepper
1 onion, chopped, or ½ cup	mayonnaise to bind
chopped scallions	

Chop up the eggs and blend with the other ingredients. Makes 2 generous servings.

PARSLEY PATTIES

Chop and combine a generous bunch of parsley leaves, the green portion of 3 or 4 scallions (substitute onions if scallions are not available), some leftover ham, and ½ green pepper chopped. Bind together with 3 or 4 beaten eggs and add seasoning. Fry on an oiled skillet like pancakes. The greens, not the eggs, should predominate in the patties. A little chopped fresh dill will give the patties a piquant flavor.

I almost forgot: Plant Italian parsley, not the curly variety, which is more decorative than edible. At least, we find it harder to chew.

If you have a garden, do plant garlic segments. The greens are delicious in salads. So what if your friends keep a safe distance! Chew parsley.

Planting garlic is easy. Take a store-bought garlic bulb, separate it into cloves, and plant each root end down about 2 inches under the soil. Your new bulbs will be ready to harvest when the greens turn yellow.

For salads or flavoring, the greens may be snipped off anytime, but leave some to feed sun to the bulb. Plant garlic near tomatoes and peppers to keep the bugs away.

It's time to pick grape leaves, now at their tender best, for wrapping into two delectable Near Eastern dishes, one with meat and one without.

I took to the road again for the two areas nearby where the most tender grape leaves grow by the roadside. Usually, I spend two or three days trying to pick enough for winter use, too, for I like to freeze a supply. I quit early, though, after trying to fight off swarms of bloodthirsty mosquitoes.

In my youth, we made family trips to the country looking for wild grapevines with tender leaves, and everybody picked. Before freezers, my mother bottled the surplus leaves in salt water.

Bottled leaves are available in gourmet and large food stores now, but it's much more fun to pick your own. Stuffed grape leaves are so delicious and easy to make that I urge everyone to take a trip to the country en famille, brave the mosquitoes, and pick a supply. Avoid the leaves that are coarse and have white backs. They're tough. Look for thinner leaves with the back slightly lighter in shade than the front. The children won't be much help, but they will enjoy the family outing, the clean country air, the songs of birds, the croak of frogs, and the chirp of chipmunks, all lavishly at their peak at this time.

When picking, I snip the leaves off with short stems, using my thumbnail. The stems facilitate separation later, before use. Stack the leaves one on top of the other in piles of about twenty-five. I roll up each such bunch during picking and circle it with a rubber band.

People driving by give me quizzical looks and probably think I'm crazy, especially when they spot my zany sunbonnet. My current favorite is a faded Italian straw resembling the one Chico Marx wore in the Marx brothers comedies. I think it looked better on Chico. Anyhow, I just grin at the "city folk" and keep on stacking my grape leaves.

Each stack is blanched by placing in salt water and boiling for about two minutes on each side; after cooling, roll up again, wring out, then wrap in plastic wrap. (Discard the rubber band before blanching. The stack will not separate.) Put all the bundles in one large plastic or paper bag, label it, and store in the freezer.

When needed, the bundles thaw out promptly if placed in warm water. I wring them out again before separating them for stuffing.

To use fresh-picked leaves, blanch them and wring out as for freezing. I line the heavy pot I use to cook the stuffed leaves with a layer of leaves, and separate a few at a time for stuffing, draping them on the rim of the pot.

In addition to grape leaves, cabbage leaves, tomatoes, and peppers can be stuffed with the folllowing meat stuffing. Although grape and cabbage leaves are stuffed separately, stuffed tomatoes and peppers are cooked together in one pot. Zucchini is sometimes stuffed and cooked with the tomatoes and peppers.

MEAT STUFFING

1½ pounds fatty ground lamb or beef, or mixture of both	½ cup chopped fresh parsley or ¼ cup dry parsley
¾ cup raw rice	1 cup canned tomatoes
1 cup chopped onions	salt and pepper to taste

Combine all ingredients with the hands into a sloppy mixture.

Usually I substitute ¼ cup coarse ground bulgur for the same amount of rice. How about adding a handful of wheat germ to the stuffing? It never occurred to me to try this before, but I shall do so next time.

STUFFED GRAPE LEAVES

Tagak

Shape a portion of stuffing into a small cylinder, and place it on a leaf near the stem end after pinching off the remaining piece of stem. Fold down the lobes near the stem, fold in the sides, and roll toward the point of the leaf. Arrange the stuffed leaves side by side in a heavy pot, making as many layers as necessary.

I use my hands for the whole operation, but the leaf may be placed on a dish and stuffed. You may have only 2 layers if a large heavy skillet is used, but more layers if a smaller utensil is used.

Pour 2 cups of canned tomatoes over the stuffed leaves; and add more salt if necessary and about ½ cup water. Cover, bring to a boil, lower heat, and let simmer about 1 hour. I test for doneness by tasting one, sometimes two and three. Makes 40 to 50 cylinders and serves 4 to 8, depending on whether the stuffed leaves are served as a whole meal or side dish. We consider them, as well as the stuffed cabbage leaves and other stuffed vegetables, the main dish and include a salad or sweet corn and perhaps a quick bread or rolls. I freeze the extra quantity to serve as a side dish and impress guests.

STUFFED CABBAGE LEAVES

Sarma

To prepare the cabbage leaves, cut out and discard the core of a large head, almost cover rest of head with water in a deep pot, and parboil. Peel off the outer leaves as they become flexible.

When the cabbage is cool, cut the largest leaves in half, removing the hard center stem and the large stem section near the core on the other leaves. Eat some, and throw the rest in the bottom of the cooking pot. Fill with the same meat stuffing as for grape leaves. Again, start rolling from the core end of the leaf, but don't turn in the sides. You will have large rolls, not as neat as the grape-leaf cylinders, in taste and appearance somewhat like the Polish *golabki.* Makes 10 to 20 cabbage rolls for 4 to 6 servings.

STUFFED TOMATOES AND PEPPERS

Dolma

To prepare the tomatoes, slit them across the top without cutting through, to make a hinged cover. Scoop out the insides with a small spoon, and use the scoopings in the stuffing (see Meat Stuffing) instead of canned tomatoes. When cooking, also omit the 2 cups of canned tomatoes and substitute water.

Slit around the top of the peppers, grasp the stem, push in, and pull out. The seeds and a rim of pepper will be attached to the stem. Peel off the rim, eat it, save it for a salad, or throw it into the bottom of the pot.

Stuff the peppers and arrange them and the largest stuffed tomatoes in the bottom layer of the pot; put the rest of the stuffed tomatoes on top. Add salt and water, and cook in the same manner as the stuffed grape and cabbage leaves. Makes 10 to 15 stuffed tomatoes and peppers, depending on size.

The other gourmet dish with grape leaves calls for a stuffing with rice, herbs, and nuts. It is usually served cold, which makes it a dandy food for hot weather eating. It is a fine hors d'oeuvre, too, and that's how I serve it to guests, who look forward to this treat.

GRAPE LEAVES STUFFED
WITH RICE, HERBS, AND NUTS
Yolonchi

3 large onions, chopped	¼ teaspoon cinnamon
1¼ cups corn or olive oil	¼ teaspoon paprika
2 cups raw rice	⅓ cup pignolia nuts or
½ to 1 cup fresh chopped	other broken nut meats
parsley	⅓ cup seedless raisins
4 tablespoons fresh chopped dill	juice of 1 lemon
fronds	1 tablespoon honey or sugar
1 tablespoon fresh chopped basil	2 cups water
1 tablespoon fresh chopped mint	salt and pepper to taste

In a large heavy skillet, sauté the onions in oil for about 2 minutes. Add the other ingredients, cover, and cook gently for about 10 minutes until the water is absorbed. Put aside until cold, or make the stuffing the day before and refrigerate.

Line a heavy pot with grape leaves. This food especially has a tendency to stick to the bottom, since—in the final cooking—most or all liquid should be absorbed. If the grape leaves are limited in quantity, place a low trivet in the bottom of the pot or skillet during the final cooking.

This stuffing is more difficult to manage than the meat stuffing, and it helps to save the largest leaves for it. I spoon some stuffing on each leaf. After all the leaves are stuffed, squeeze the juice of another lemon over all, sprinkle with more salt, and add 2½ cups water. Simmer about 1 hour—until most of the liquid is absorbed and the contents cooked. Makes about 100 stuffed leaves, which I have seen disappear at a cocktail party in half an hour.

I always use brown rice in this recipe for extra nutrition. Since brown rice takes longer to cook, I parboil it in 3 cups of water first. When I add it to the other stuffing ingredients, I reduce the water from 2 cups to 1 cup. For the final cooking, I reduce the water by half, from 2½ to 1¼ cups.

In the stuffing, use about a fourth of the quantity if only dried herbs are available. When serving, garnish with thin lemon slices.

Since this recipe makes a large quantity, invite a friend or relative to help you wrap and make a fun event of the project. Other recipes with meat stuffing freeze well in broth, but these hors d'oeuvres do not. However, they keep well for about two weeks in the refrigerator.

None of these recipes is as difficult as it may sound. I have gone into much detail so that you will be acclaimed a gourmet cook the first time you try them. At first, wrapping the leaves will take most of your time, but with experience you will become more proficient. These tasty, nutritious recipes will help you add variety to your menus.

Until fresh vegetables become available, our vitamins come from the freezer supply. I have long since adopted the Far Eastern style of cooking vegetables for only a few minutes in as little water as possible, to retain the crisp flavor and to preserve the vitamins. Far Eastern cooks sauté vegetables in oil, but we usually forego this luxury because of our tendency to gain weight at the least indulgence.

The Japanese also serve tempuras or batter-fried foods. Here is a vegetable tempura that is easy to make and can also be used for small pieces of fish or lobster meat.

VEGETABLE TEMPURA

Make a batter by beating 1 egg with ½ cup cold water. Add ¼ teaspoon salt and enough flour for a thin batter. I use stone-ground whole wheat flour.

Cut the vegetables very thin and see that they are thoroughly dry. Use eggplant, butternut squash, carrots, mushrooms, green beans, mild onions, and green peppers.

Heat about 1 inch of oil in a skillet. Using a slotted spoon, dip the vegetables in batter, then cook them in oil a few at a time, so that the temperature of the oil does not drop.

BLOSSOM TEMPURA

For the cook who has served nearly everything and wants a gourmet touch of something different, milkweed flowers, elderberry blossoms, and male squash flowers may also be cooked in this manner when in season. On the squash plants, the female flowers turn into squash. Check the stem end to differentiate them.

We had a busy day after the weather bureau predicted a late frost because I had already put out most of my plants.

I got home late to find George in the doorway of the barn wrestling with the assembly of a new power lawn mower to replace our sick fifteen-year-old one, which had finally gasped its last. "I think some of the screws are missing," he said, picking up the directions.

We have a riding mower, too, but need a small mower to get under the branches of fruit trees and in other narrow spaces.

George was determined this year to keep ahead of our acre of lawn, but the two mowers took turns dropping dead for reasons beyond George's ken. He finally decided the old hand power mower had succumbed from old age, so went into town and bought a new one.

"Some of the screws are missing all right, but I'm not so sure they're from the mower," I said, giving him a quick glance to see if he had lost his sense of humor during the assembly. He laughed.

"How about giving me a hand to cover the plants?" I asked. "The forecast predicts frost."

I had a few Hotkaps, but they were enough to cover only about half the plants. We both remembered the small plastic pails at the same time. We have about twenty of them in pastel shades. Sometimes they cost as little as ten cents each on sale; at the next sale, I shall buy twenty or thirty more.

We inverted them over the remaining plants in no time flat. George weighted them down with stones, of which we have an unlimited quantity, to insure their stability. The garden took on a strange appearance, dotted with pails of various hues.

I had a few plants tied to tall stakes by the stone wall near the swale. They had me stumped for a while, but I thought of an effective way to cover them too. I used large, heavy paper shopping bags, in which I pierced holes big enough to fit over the stakes as I inverted the bags and slid them down over the plants.

Earlier in the week, when I had put the tomato and pimiento plants in the garden, I remembered to spread wood ashes around them to keep the cutworms away, and this method of controlling the cutworms had worked again. Not one plant had been cut down.

For dinner, I made stewed onions with apricots, a foreign combination I stopped making after the price of dried apricots zoomed up. However, George said last week he would shell out for the apricots if I made it, and he came home from town one day with a boxful. Although this mixture may seem weird, it is so delicious you will have to eat it to be convinced.

STEWED ONIONS AND APRICOTS

30 small onions, peeled	½ teaspoon cinnamon
½ cup water or broth	¼ teaspoon paprika
1 tablespoon corn oil	15 dried apricot halves
salt and pepper	

Combine the onions, water or broth, oil, spices, and seasoning in a pot, cover, and simmer until the onions are almost cooked. Add the apricots and simmer a little longer. Serve as a vegetable course. Makes 6 to 7 servings.

The temperature rose to 90° one day! I quickly made Green Lime Ice Cream.

This recipe started out to be Florida's famous Key lime pie, which —naturally enough—is made with Key limes. I never tasted Key limes, but I saw some once which, to me, looked like sick lemons, being yellow instead of green.

In March, while vacationing in Miami, we took a trip down to the Florida Keys. Jan, our daughter-in-law, who was eating for two, stopped the car at a very nautical lunchroom complete with a cursing parrot.

I wasn't going to eat at all, having strained my diet until I was afraid to get weighed, but then I noticed Key lime pie on the menu. Thinking: What better place to eat this delicacy than in the Keys? I ordered a piece. The waitress-owner said she was fresh out, but when she discovered I was a cooking enthusiast, she offered to give me her recipe. It didn't take a supersleuth to track that down, as I'm a chummy sort and have a big mouth.

Limes were on sale for five cents each one day after we returned, so I decided to try the pie without a crust (to cut the calories), and call it Green Lime Pudding. At first, I wasn't impressed with the flavor of the pudding, which I tasted without refrigerating it or letting it set. So I spooned most of the mixture into plastic cups and put them in the freezer. And that's how I discovered Green Lime Ice Cream.

GREEN LIME ICE CREAM

4 eggs, separated	1 14-ounce can sweetened
2 limes, juice and grated rind	condensed milk

Beat the 4 egg yolks and 1 egg white until thick. Add the juice and rind of the limes and the condensed milk. Stir. Fold in the remaining egg whites beaten stiff. Freeze. Makes about a pint.

In summer, frozen treats are most welcome. The easiest wholesome refresher is pure fruit juice frozen in plastic containers. I stay alive through muggy hot spells by eating frozen pineapple juice. I simply pour the unsweetened juice into containers and freeze. When our children were small, I made pineapple juice Popsicles for them, but for myself I just hack the frozen lump into pieces.

Here are more easy frozen treats.

FRUIT FREEZE

1 tablespoon gelatin	1 cup pineapple juice
¾ cup water	1 cup crushed pineapple
¾ cup frozen orange juice concentrate	3 tablespoons lemon juice

Soften the gelatin in water. Heat to dissolve, and add the orange juice concentrate. Stir in the other ingredients and freeze. Makes about 1 quart.

GRAPE JUICE OR ORANGE JUICE ICE CREAM

1 cup grape juice or orange juice	1 cup cream
juice of ½ lemon	1 cup sugar or honey

Add the lemon juice to the grape juice or orange juice. Beat the cream until stiff. Continue beating and add the mixed juices alternately with the sugar or honey. Freeze. Makes nearly 1 quart.

BERRY OR FRUIT MOUSSE

1 quart berries or fruit	⅔ cup honey or sugar
2 egg whites	juice of 1 lemon
⅔ cup water	2 tablespoons brandy (optional)
⅔ cup powdered milk	

Beat the egg whites, water, and powdered milk together to form peaks. Blend the other ingredients and add them gradually. Fold in the mashed fruit or berries last. Chill. Makes 6 to 8 servings.

FRUIT SHERBET

1 lemon	1 banana, mashed
1 orange	1 cup sugar or honey
1 cup mashed berries or fruit	1 cup light cream or milk

Juice the lemon and orange. Blend the juice with the other ingredients. Freeze, stirring once during the freezing process. Makes nearly 1 quart.

BERRY ICE

1 tablespoon gelatin	2 cups berries
¼ cup cold water	¾ cup honey or sugar
1 cup boiling water	

Soften the gelatin in cold water. Dissolve the mixture in boiling water and cool. Whiz the berries in the blender. Add honey or sugar and the gelatin, and stir. Freeze in ice cube trays, inserting sticks for pops, if desired. Makes about 1 quart.

Here is a doozy for health nuts:

CAROB ICE CREAM

1 cup soya powder	½ cup corn oil
1 cup cold water	2 egg yolks
½ cup carob powder	2 teaspoons vanilla
1 cup honey	

Put the ingredients in a blender in the order listed and whiz hard after each is added. Beat once during freezing. Makes about 1 quart.

I buy bulk gelatin by mail for a fraction of the cost of the measured envelopes. One tablespoon is equivalent to one envelope. When using the bulk form, I add a little more to insure a firmer gelatin, especially if I use juicy fruits.

In addition to using gelatin in frozen treats, I make my own pure gelatin desserts and sometimes use it to thicken fruit cocktail into a fruit gelatin. It is very nutritious in its unadulterated form and adds body to many foods.

This easy pure gelatin dessert is a favorite.

PURE GELATIN DESSERT

2 tablespoons unflavored gelatin	½ cup honey or sugar (about)
3 cups fruit juice	few drops Angostura bitters (optional)

Sprinkle the gelatin over 1 cup of the fruit juice in a bowl. Heat the other 2 cups of juice, and add them and the honey or sugar. Add the bitters, if used, and a little lemon juice if the fruit juice is bland. Stir until the gelatin dissolves. Add cut fruit if desired. Serves 4 to 6.

My broccoli is late this year because I used old seeds and most didn't germinate in the peat pots on the porch. I finally bought fresh seeds and planted them directly in the garden. I can still hear George —"If you weren't so stingy . . ." I must admit I am parsimonious.

Recently I was making antipasto while Babe and Judy were visiting. Babe was in the kitchen with me.

As I turned the key to open the anchovy fillets can, the oil squirted in my face and eyes in spite of my glasses. I ran to the sink to rinse out my burning eyes as Babe finished opening the can and sniffed at the fish.

"I think this can is spoiled," he said. "Don't use it."

"Give it to Axel and Ed," I said. Axel and Ed are our cats.

Babe looked at me, horrified. "Suppose they get poisoned?"

"Then we'll know the fillets were spoiled."

He turned, shook his head from side to side, and started for the rubbish container in the utility room with the can.

"Hold it!" I yelled. "Give it to the worms."

He returned and emptied the fish into the garbage pail.

Subconsciously, I knew he wouldn't risk the lives of our cats and neither would I. My initial reaction was undoubtedly instinctive. Inherent traits are difficult to overcome. Early in life I was told I took after my penny-pinching grandmother on my mother's side.

I haven't had a chance to get a refund on that can yet ...

July

ONE OF THE reasons we selected our farm home among several others was that we were told a picturesque lake and beach were "down the road a piece."

The boys and I were here without George during our first summer and we had no car. We didn't consider that a hardship, however, as there was unlimited exploring to be done on and around the farm. Besides, a friendly neighbor at walking distance offered to take us to town for shopping whenever she went on her butter and egg route, which was at least once a week.

One hot and humid day, the boys, six and eight years old then, begged me to take them to the beach at the lake. I resisted as long as I could, since we had never been any distance down the road pointed out to us as the direction to the beach, and I had no idea just how far it was. I found out the hard way, probably because my idea of walking distance and what others here considered walking distance did not coincide, especially in such hot weather.

I finally gave in to the boys' pleading and got into my bathing suit while they put on their trunks. We each took a towel and hit the road, which—in those days—was dirt. By the time we got to the second farmhouse after trudging what seemed miles, we decided to stop and ask further directions and beg drinking water, as we were parched from the intense heat.

A nice lady vacationing from New York City gave us water and told us we were on course—to bear right when we reached the end of the road and keep going until we saw the lake. Later, when I reviewed that adventure, I couldn't believe she didn't warn me that it was a distance of at least two miles, and much too far to walk with two little half-naked boys under such a hot sun.

We hit the road again and trudged on. Soon we were thirsty again —the kind of thirst that must happen in deserts, but the mirage we saw finally turned out to be an honest-to-goodness brook, running with crystal-clear water. Having no container, we cupped our hands and slurped enough water to come alive again. Then we flopped on a grassy bank under a tree to reconnoiter our position.

The boys did not want to turn back. Their reasoning was that since we had come so far, the beach must be just ahead—and how good the water would feel after the hot walk! Since they were the majority, I lost and on we went. We finally hit the end of the road, turned right, and dragged on until we hit N.H. 11. On and on we went until, in the distance on our left, beyond a railroad track, we saw the lake.

But where was the beach? Again I flopped down on a grassy bank, on the verge of collapse, under a tree off the highway. I told the boys I had reached the end of the line. And besides, I had no idea where the beach was or how to get to it, and no one was around to ask.

Perhaps I did look done in because they didn't protest but sat down beside me. We rested about fifteen minutes and started back. We were again plagued by thirst, slurped water at the brook, and stopped at the New York lady's house for more. Being chicken, I did not berate her about the distance. When we finally reached home and had sufficiently recovered, we filled one of the galvanized tubs that had come with the farm with water from our well via a pitcher pump and bucket, and the boys cooled off.

I turned several shades darker while gardening during the long Fourth of July weekend. We picked edible pod snow peas and several heads of cos lettuce, both welcome additions to our salads. Other vegetables now available from the garden are chard, beet greens, and tiny carrots, the last two through thinning in the rows. In the herb garden, we have been picking scallions, mint, chives, and sage.

A young couple who went back to the land to grow their own food visited us to look over our garden. They said theirs was in poor condition because of the prolonged dry spell, and they were envious to find our plants lush and healthy. Under the hay in the rows, our soil was moist and wormy.

The only excuse for not having an organic garden, in my opinion, is lack of hay or other mulch materials. However, in most areas leaves are available from neighbors or city highway departments. Wood chips and sawdust can also be used, although sawdust may cause nitrogen deficiency.

If your soil is not very fertile, watch for nitrogen deficiency, which can be detected if your plants turn light green or yellow. Then side dress under the mulch with an organic fertilizer, such as cottonseed meal, compost, or manure.

Another way to keep moisture in the soil is to use a newspaper mulch. Put several thicknesses or sections between the rows and weight them down with rocks or soil.

A woodchuck invaded our garden and harvested some of our snow peas. I don't think we will see him or any member of his family again. I don't shoot woodchucks anymore. I find it more efficient to track them to their burrows and gas them humanely. I don't like to do this, but know of no other way to cope with the problem. Some of the cucumber plants were nipped too, but will revive, albeit a little late.

This is the time to make a stick-to-the-ribs lima bean salad, especially suited to hot weather eating.

LIMA BEAN SALAD

Piaz

Cook, drain, and cool lima beans in any quantity desired. Guided by taste, add chopped scallions or chives, dill fronds, parsley, and green pepper. Combine 2 parts oil with 1 part vinegar, and add to taste, or use French dressing. Season with salt and pepper and toss together until blended. I use about 1 cup of chopped herbs to 2 cups of lima beans. Serve on lettuce with sliced tomatoes.

When good tomatoes are not in season, I often make a salad of greens only. My family calls it

GRASS SALAD

Tear or cut up any greens available. I have at various times included sorrel, dandelion greens, beet greens, collards, scallions, chives, young chard leaves, parsley, dill fronds, cress, spinach leaves, cauliflowerets, shredded cabbage, zucchini, celery, radish greens, and lettuce. After seasoning with salt, I toss with garlic dressing or my mother's original French dressing.

To make the garlic dressing, combine 2 parts oil to 1 part vinegar, add ¼ teaspoon tarragon and 1 kernel garlic. Let set at least one day.

My mother concocted this French dressing when she was cooking professionally for a noted restaurant on Block Island years ago. The restaurant advertised it as its own famous dressing.

FRENCH DRESSING

1 cup corn, olive, or salad oil	¼ teaspoon dry mustard
½ cup cider vinegar	¼ teaspoon horseradish powder
½ teaspoon salt	1 teaspoon Worcestershire sauce
2 tablespoons honey or sugar	¼ cup ketchup
juice of ½ lemon	1 or 2 shakes Tabasco
½ small onion, grated	1 small clove garlic (optional)

Combine all the ingredients in a container, shake well, and let stand overnight. Shake again before use.

While we are on the subject of dressings, here is a dandy one for fruit salad.

YOGURT DRESSING

1 cup plain yogurt	1 tablespoon lemon juice
2 tablespoons mayonnaise	½ teaspoon salt
2 tablespoons honey or sugar	1 teaspoon grenadine syrup (optional)

Blend all the ingredients and refrigerate until used.

Purslane, an excellent green, is discarded as a weed by most gardeners. I miss it since we went into organic gardening and mulching. Before, we looked for it among the weeds and put it aside for later use.

In my youth, I remember my mother buying purslane for fifty cents a bushel from Armenian farmers at the farmers' market. It was highly prized by those in the know as a versatile and nutritious green. When I introduced farmers to it after we moved here, I discovered they called it "pussley" and considered it a real garden pest.

Purslane, a member of the portulaca family, originated in India or Persia, according to Euell Gibbons in *Stalking the Wild Asparagus.* Among its other virtues is its high iron content.

This succulent plant hugs the ground as it spreads through tentacles. I learned from Gibbons that if the leafy tips are pinched off, new ones will replace them, a few plants furnishing a continuous supply. My supply, however, comes from neighboring gardens now, where I offer to weed out the purslane. I take the greens home, cut off the roots and cut the fleshy stems into pieces, then wash them thoroughly.

If I pick a large supply, I freeze some. First I steam the greens for a few minutes in as little water as possible until they wilt. Then I spread the purslane on trays over a trivet to cool fast before packaging it. Here are some fine purslane recipes.

PURSLANE SALAD

Steam washed and cut purslane in a little water until cooked. Drain and cool. Add slivered onions, chopped parsley, cut-up fresh tomatoes, a little chopped fresh dill fronds and basil (if available), salt, pepper, and oil and vinegar or French dressing. Toss and eat.

PURSLANE WITH GRAINS

1 chopped onion	2 cups chicken broth,
2 tablespoons each	soup stock, or water
butter and corn oil	2 to 3 cups washed and
1 cup coarse bulgur	cut purslane

Sauté the onion in the butter and oil for 2 or 3 minutes in a heavy pot or large skillet. Add the bulgur, stirring to coat each grain, then the liquid. Cover the pot and cook until the liquid is almost absorbed. Add the purslane and finish cooking. Season with salt and pepper. Hulled wheat can be substituted for the bulgur, but increase the liquid to 2½ cups and cook twice as long, about 1 hour. Makes about 4 servings.

Purslane may also be steamed, seasoned, and served with butter. Or use it in any recipe in place of other greens.

PURSLANE WITH VEGETABLES

1 large onion, slivered
3 tablespoons corn oil
1 quart washed and cut purslane

2 cups canned or fresh peeled
  and cut tomatoes

Sauté the onion for about 5 minutes in oil; add purslane and tomatoes, and cook about 10 minutes or until done. Season. Makes 3 to 5 servings.

Red raspberries are ripe.

I never gave it much thought before, but during the past few years, I have slowly come to the realization that I like to pick berries of all kinds. I like to be among the bushes in the clean countryside where only the bucolic sounds of summer surround me—the song of birds, the isolated croak of a frog, or insects buzzing around my head. (I could do without the buzzing insects.)

While I pick, I have a chance to unwind, to meditate and gradually calm down from the stimulating turmoil of my working day. On rare occasions when I pick wild blueberries, I manage to squeeze in a little exploring, too. I love the long languid summer days. There are many advantages to living on a farm in the country. The chief drawback is the distance traveled during hazardous winter months.

I digress—back to the berries:

My first stop, after getting home from work, is the berry patch. I pick into one of my homemade buckets, hung around my neck to free both hands. These are made by completely removing one end of a large juice can and filing or sanding off any rough spots on the rim. Using a nail, I punch holes on each side of the opening with a hammer, and fasten a strong cord long enough for looping around my neck, through the holes. In the past, when I had time, I painted the outside of the cans and applied free-hand designs.

Usually I eat my fill as I pick, getting a maximum of vitamins and curbing my hunger for less nutritious foods. Why not, I rationalize? Didn't I plant the raspberry patch? I'm merely reaping what I sowed, I think smugly.

If berries are available in quantity, I think they should be eaten out of hand when picked. Since everyone does not have a berry patch, here are my two favorite berry dessert recipes.

RASPBERRY ROLL

4 eggs
¾ cup honey or sugar
1 cup flour
2 tablespoons powdered milk
(optional)

2 teaspoons baking powder
¼ teaspoon baking soda
½ teaspoon vanilla
confectioners' sugar

(If sugar is used instead of honey, add 2 tablespoons milk to the batter and omit the baking soda.)

Beat the eggs until very light, then add the honey. Combine the dry ingredients and add them to the egg mixture. Add vanilla. Bake in a 15½ x 10½ inch jelly roll pan, which has been lined with wax paper, at 350° for about 25 minutes.

Meanwhile, sprinkle a clean cloth towel with confectioners' sugar. Immediately invert the cake onto the towel; gently remove the wax paper. Roll cake and towel from the narrow end, and cool the roll completely on a trivet. Unroll and spread with raspberry filling; reroll without the towel.

RASPBERRY FILLING

1 quart raspberries
½ to ¾ cup sugar

small pinch salt
4 tablespoons cornstarch

Crush the raspberries, add sugar and salt, and bring to a boil. Stir in the cornstarch dissolved in a little water, and simmer 1 minute more. Cool completely before spreading.

BLUEBERRY COBBLER

1 quart blueberries sweetened
with ½ cup honey or sugar
2 cups flour
2 teaspoons baking powder
1 teaspoon salt
2 tablespoons powdered milk
(optional)

⅔ cup sugar or honey
2 eggs
½ cup milk
4 tablespoons corn oil
1 teaspoon vanilla

Cover the bottom of a large baking pan, 15 x 10 x 2 inches, with sweetened berries. Combine the dry ingredients in a mixing bowl. Beat the eggs, milk, oil, and vanilla, and fold the liquid into the dry ingredients. Spread the mixture over the berries and bake in 350° oven about 40 minutes. Invert to remove. Serve with ice cream, cream, or plain yogurt.

I may have said this before, but I repeat—I use only unbleached white flour and often substitute, for one half or for all of it, stone-ground whole wheat flour. The idea is to get back to baking with wholesome ingredients. I recommend this method. You may get some flak from your family unless you introduce the change gradually, since we have all been conditioned to dead, refined flours. But once your family begins eating wholesome foods, I'll wager they will prefer the new flavors.

I was asked recently how I find time to bake bread, make preserves, and generally fiddle in the kitchen in addition to my outside work. I don't. I *make* time, since to me cooking is a creative, exciting, and relaxing pursuit, as rewarding as any other arts and crafts.

There is one drawback. To discover whether a new creation is a success, naturally I must taste it. Usually I find myself going overboard—overeating and sometimes increasing my size. Then I go through a period of repentance by staying out of the kitchen and relaxing through creative sewing, rugmaking, embroidering, or anything else that will keep my mind off food. Guess what happened to the leftover half glass of pink marmalade last week?

I had no intention of making marmalade but Gail brought home some large, thick-skinned oranges, perfect marmalade fruit. I couldn't resist.

PINK MARMALADE

I cut 3 unpeeled oranges and 3 lemons in quarters lengthwise, and then cut the quarters into very thin slices. Into a large pot, along with the citrus slices, I put a quart of our own raspberries and barely enough water to cover, and simmered the mixture covered for about 10 minutes. Next addition was part honey and part sugar, to taste. This time I let the mixture boil hard, uncovered, to the jelling stage. After pouring the marmalade into glasses, I topped each with melted paraffin.

I should explain here that the usual recipes call for the same amount of sugar as fruit by measure. We like our preserves tart, so I go by taste and usually add a cup or two less sugar than fruit. Works fine, and makes it easier to overindulge when tasting.

Our jam and jelly supply was nearly gone, mostly given away, so later, when I was making bread one day, I decided to throw together a batch of plum jam to use up some of last year's fruit from our trees, still in the freezer. (The fruit, that is.)

MAROON JAM

I had sliced the plums into quart containers, added honey, and stirred to meld, before freezing them, Now, after emptying 3 of these quart containers into a large kettle to make the jam, I was about to cut a lemon to add for more tang and pectin when I remembered I had frozen rhubarb in my other freezer (we keep a small spare freezer in the cellar for overflow). So I added 1 quart container of our deep pink strawberry rhubarb instead.

When the mixture had simmered a few minutes, I turned up the burner to bring it to a fast boil, added sugar and honey to taste as usual, and finished the jam the same way I did the Pink Marmalade. Our strawberry rhubarb and reddish purple plums turned into a maroon-hued preserve of delectable flavor. Fortunately for me, there was very little left over to taste, after the glasses had been filled.

I recommend making jam from frozen fruit to eliminate the process of preparing the fruit the same day and to get preserves made in record time. When time is limited, it also helps to have a husband or family who likes jam and is willing to collect and wash the glasses.

Through experience, I have discovered that nearly every kind of fruit and berries can be combined successfully to make delicious jams and jellies. The trick is to use at least one fruit with sufficient pectin, or use bottled pectin. It is also necessary to learn to recognize the jelling stage—when the mixture sheets off a spoon.

Although my preserves win prizes now, I reached this point the hard way. I palmed off my first grape-elderberry jelly on the family as a new exotic syrup for pancakes and waffles because I had miscalculated the jelling stage. Also, the elderberries predominated, and they are noted for their lack of pectin.

This combination makes an unusually fine-flavored jelly. Take a family trip into the country in the fall and pick both these fruits by the roadsides. Use more grape juice than elderberry juice for enough pectin. I found some crab apples on the ground in an old field across from our farm, so used about one cup of crab-apple juice, rich in pectin, with the other juices.

GRAPE-ELDERBERRY JELLY

Pick the grapes and berries from the clusters. Wash them, then bring to a boil with about 1 inch of water in the bottom of the pot. Simmer for about 15 minutes, crushing the fruit. Put the pulp in a cheesecloth bag and hang it over a large pan or bowl while the juice drips out.

Measure the juice, then bring it to a boil in a large pot. Add an equal amount of sugar, or less for more tartness, and ½ bottle of pectin. Boil hard to the jelling stage, skim, and pour into glasses, topping them with paraffin.

I did a heap of strawberry picking one weekend after Ozzie at Hillside Orchards gave me permission to scrounge in one of his strawberry patches before he cut it down. I moved through that patch with my head to the ground for so long, I could hardly straighten up. Fortunately, I recovered within a day or so, a feat I attribute to my return to Yoga postures, neglected for more than a year. I returned to daily Yoga when I noticed my joints giving in to old age.

Besides freezing a quantity of berries, I made 12 glasses of jam by this method.

TART STRAWBERRY JAM

I added 6 cups of sugar to 8 cups of mashed berries in a large pot, and stirred until the mixture went into a hard boil. Then I added ½ bottle of pectin, and boiled the fruit to the jelling stage. After pouring the jam into glasses, I topped them with paraffin.

I might as well admit that I broke down and made old-fashioned strawberry shortcake, too, when I discovered that old-fashioned heavy cream was available from a neighboring farmer. My, was that ever good!

OLD-FASHIONED STRAWBERRY SHORTCAKE

1½ cups flour (unsifted)
4 tablespoons powdered milk
  (optional)
1 tablespoon baking powder
½ teaspoon salt

2 tablespoons sugar or honey
4 tablespoons corn oil
1 beaten egg
⅔ cup milk

Stir dry ingredients with a fork in a bowl. Combine oil, egg, milk, and honey if used and fold into dry ingredients. Spoon into six round globs on baking sheet and bake in 400° oven about 15 minutes.

Beat heavy cream with sugar or honey to taste until stiff. Slice strawberries in a bowl and meld with honey or sugar to sweetness desired.

Split cooled shortcakes. Spoon cream and strawberries on bottom half. Cover with top half and pile more cream and berries over top. The shortcake is sometimes buttered, too, but we feel we don't need the extra calories.

When making the shortcake, I substitute ¼ cup each soy powder and wheat germ for ½ cup of the flour and use unbleached flour.

Our house must be the only one around that features bouquets of dead flowers. They're alive when I arrange them throughout the house, but when I'm at work George never replenishes the water in vases as it evaporates, and suddenly I find the rooms festooned with dead bouquets. If I don't use some of my hoarded spare time to throw them out, they stay indefinitely. I have subtly told George to feel free to throw the bouquets away after the flowers die, since I lose interest at that point. He doesn't take the hint.

Finally, I figured out why there was such a large space between the carrot and beet rows: George eradicated one row of beets. That space puzzled me for a long time until I noticed one beet plant in the center, which had managed to struggle through the hay mulch. When I planted that end of the garden, George offered to mulch between the rows. He apparently missed that row.

While I'm complaining, I might as well bring up another frustration. George takes one look at some of the concoctions I put together and refuses even to taste them. To understand why, one must realize that he is so straight it spills over to his eating habits. When I married him, he was strictly a sausage, peas, and mashed potatoes hash-house eater. He has come a long way since then, but not all the way.

I get pretty irked when he gives me that "whoever heard of eating salad with scrambled eggs?" routine, or when he glances at what I consider some of my best food combinations, shakes his head, and says, "Whoever heard of mixing all the stuff together—then eating it?" Recently I picked a few green beans, a small zucchini, and a small head of broccoli, combined them with a mild cheese, and turned out a really elegant dish. I offered George a taste, promising that if he didn't like it, I wouldn't feel hurt if he didn't eat anymore. He liked the cheesy vegetables and ate a good portion.

CHEESY VEGETABLES

Steam cut-up beans, broccoli flowerets, and sliced zucchini in a little water, beginning with the beans and broccoli, until crunchy-cooked. Drain any water left and, in a heavy large skillet, combine the vegetables with a little butter or oil or a combination of both. Add cut-up mild cheese, such as Muenster or Monterey Jack, stir until the cheese melts, and sprinkle all with fresh chopped parsley just before serving. I forgot—season with salt and pepper. Quantities are not important in this recipe. Create your own balance with the available ingredients.

Although our garden is not very large, our daily crop of vegetables seems endless. To use up some of the green peppers from our dozen plants, I roasted several. Most homemakers fry peppers, but we find roasting them tastier and lower calories.

ROASTED PEPPERS

Place the peppers under the broiler in the oven; turn them frequently for an even roast. Peel off the burnt skin, add salt, and serve them hot or cold. Two or three peppers may be roasted on a trivet over a medium flame on a gas stove or the heating unit of an electric stove. For a cookout, roast them on a grill over hot coals.

We have been forcing fancy long green cucumbers and huge zucchini squashes on friends and neighbors. Here is a gourmet recipe with cucumbers that is very popular in Near Eastern countries.

CUCUMBERS WITH MINTED YOGURT

Beat about 1 cup of plain yogurt; add a small clove of minced garlic and a few chopped fresh mint leaves. Cover and set in the refrigerator about 1 hour to blend the flavors. Add 1 or more sliced cucumbers, depending on their size, and salt to taste. If you have the type of cucumbers we grow, some of them more than 15 inches long, one will be adequate to serve two people.

With my limited time, I find that if I use up one vegetable, others pile up in our two refrigerators. We got the extra refrigerator to indulge our passion for watermelon, which we buy whole.

The prize crop of the garden this year is cantaloupe. Before I was converted to organic gardening I had no luck with this fine fruit, so crossed it off my crop list. This year I gave in when I saw the picture of Hale's Best, Rockford-type cantaloupe, and decided to try again.

The vines grew and spread, but I had not taken the time to look under the leaves until recently. My mouth fell open when I saw all the lovely cantaloupes, but for once I was speechless. They looked exactly like the picture and almost large enough to pick! I called to George at the other end of the garden, but he wasn't a bit excited. Seems he knew it all the time. Aren't men odd?

I find myself skirting the three hills of zucchini without looking, for fear there will be a few more to pick, which accounts for their gargantuan size. Still, they are tender and delicious. But how much squash can one eat?

Zucchini, in my opinion, is the most versatile of the summer squashes. It can be cooked in the same manner as yellow summer squash and will taste as good, if not better. Picked small, zucchini will give a crunchy texture to salads, comparable to cucumbers. Here are some of our favorite recipes:

ZUCCHINI WITH TOMATOES

1 onion, slivered	1 cup canned tomatoes *or*
1 tablespoon each butter and	2 large fresh peeled tomatoes
corn oil	2 leaves fresh basil or pinch
1 medium zucchini	dried basil
salt and pepper	

In a large skillet, sauté the onion in the butter and oil mixture for 2 or 3 minutes. Add the sliced squash, tomatoes, and basil. Cover and cook, after seasoning. Makes about 3 servings.

FRIED ZUCCHINI

Slice unpeeled zucchini in ¼-inch slices, or thinner. Dip the slices in seasoned beaten egg or flour and fry in oil. Delicious! Makes 2 or 3 servings.

ZUCCHINI AU GRATIN

1 tablespoon each corn oil and butter
1 onion, slivered
1 medium zucchini
2 eggs

2 tablespoons crumbled blue cheese (optional)
½ cup cottage cheese
Flavor Salt to taste

Put the oil and butter in a large skillet, and sauté the onion and the squash, which has been cut in four pieces lengthwise and then thinly sliced. Stir occasionally until crunchy-cooked but not overcooked.

In a bowl, beat the eggs and cheeses with a fork, adding some flavor salt. Pour this over the vegetables, let the egg mixture set, and flip over by sections with a spatula. Taste, and add more flavor salt, if necessary, and some freshly ground pepper.

I use my own blend of flavor salt as seasoning. I'm sure this recipe would be delicious with grated mild hard cheese, too, but I use cottage cheese. Sometimes I omit the butter to keep calories down. Makes 2 generous servings.

BUTTERED ZUCCHINI WITH EGGS

1 medium zucchini
2 tablespoons butter

2 eggs or more
salt and pepper

Cut the squash in four pieces lengthwise and slice thin. In a heavy large skillet, steam the squash in as little water as possible until crunchy-cooked. Remove the cover and let the water evaporate if any remains, or drain the squash. Add butter and shake the skillet to spread it evenly; then add the beaten eggs and seasoning. Cook over low heat until the eggs are set, flipping over in sections once with a spatula. Makes 2 servings.

Both this recipe and Zucchini au Gratin will make a complete meal served with a salad and dessert.

For lack of cucumbers one year, I substituted zucchini in several pickle recipes calling for diced or chunked cucumbers, and got excellent results. Here is a dandy pickle I put together then. I have since given the recipe to many homemakers, even by long-distance telephone.

CRISP ZUCCHINI PICKLE

5 quarts cubed zucchini	½ cup coarse pickling salt
1 quart sliced onions	1 quart cider vinegar
1 large head cauliflower	5 cups sugar
2 green peppers	2 tablespoons mustard seed
1 quart green beans or carrots, or both	2 teaspoons celery seed
3 cloves garlic, sliced	2 teaspoons turmeric

I use two huge zucchinis, which cut up to the required amount. Split them lengthwise in strips, remove the soft center, and cube the rest. (Later, chop up the center and use it in the au gratin or egg recipe, or concoct your own combination.) Break the cauliflower into small flowerets, cut the peppers in small squares, cut up the green beans, and slice the carrots. I made this pickle originally without the beans and carrots, but one year I had some of both in the house, so threw them in—with fine results.

Combine all the vegetables and salt, cover with ice cubes, mix well, and let stand 3 hours.

In a large enamel pot, combine the vinegar, sugar, and spices. Drain the vegetables well and add them to the pot. Bring to a boil, fill hot pint jars, and seal immediately. Makes 10 to 12 pints. Chill before serving.

All vegetables are at their tender best at this time of year, and I often steam them in their skins to preserve the vitamins. Such vegetables as beets, carrots, broccoli, cauliflower, and cabbage are also delicious simmered in milk.

VEGETABLES SIMMERED IN MILK

Dice, shred, or break the vegetables in pieces. Place in a heavy skillet with ¼ to ½ cup milk; bring to a boil, stir, cover, and simmer over low heat for about 10 minutes. Season and serve.

For variety, try adding about 1 tablespoon of such herbs as mint, dill, chives, or parsley. Or omit herbs and add about ½ cup plain yogurt or sour cream before serving.

Try this fast-cooking way of serving beets.

CRUNCHY BEETS

4 cups shredded unpeeled beets	1 teaspoon corn oil
½ teaspoon lemon juice	1 teaspoon butter
salt to taste	3 tablespoons water (about)

Combine all ingredients and stir-steam until thoroughly heated and crunchy-cooked with all water evaporated. Add a little more water if necessary. Serves 4 to 6.

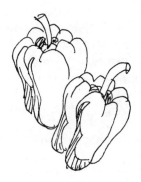

August

GEORGE and I have pitched our share of hay in the past, especially when we were raising sheep, but we never expected to be doing it at this late date, when we are both practically candidates for the rocking chair. Fact of the matter is, we have a deal with a farmer to cut all our hay, keep the field hay, and give us the hay from the area around the house to use as mulch for our garden.

The farm crew came and cut all the hay, took some, but left most of it. We anxiously awaited their return, as we were completely out of mulch hay and planned to use a bit in the fall to cover the garden.

Finally, one day George said, "I don't think they are going to pick up that hay."

I nearly panicked, since I figured he was right. At first I thought, because of the daily showers, the farmer was waiting for the cut hay to dry again, but there it still sat every day when I returned from the office.

One weekend I suggested we get the bull rake out and pick up some around the house ourselves, getting Gail to help. Unfortunately, I picked an inopportune time—right in the middle of a ball game George was watching on television.

I called Gail at her camp next door, and she said friends had dropped in from Vermont to visit. I suggested she bring them, too, since we had extra pitchforks—then went back to bull raking.

George grumbled so much as he pitched the hay into our pickup that I told him to go back to the ball game—Gail would be here soon and we would do it.

He just kept pitching, grumbling and perspiring profusely, until I was afraid he was going to drop dead. I pleaded with him to leave, and he finally did just as Gail and her friends, a young couple, arrived.

Together, we collected three truckloads, and then the bull rake snapped in two, which left us no easy means to windrow. We quit. I was so grateful that I served iced drinks and nutty macaroons.

Long after the ball game, while I was typing on the porch, George came in, in a jovial mood, and called from the kitchen: "Well, honey, I got another load of hay in!"

I gnashed my teeth and bit into a cucumber, wondering why women are considered unpredictable.

To take my mind off things, I combined green beans with edible pod snow peas that were missed by the woodchuck in our garden, and made a new vegetable dish.

GREEN BEANS AND SNOW PEAS

1 onion, slivered	2 cups green beans
1 tablespoon each corn oil and butter	2 cups snow peas
¼ cup water	chopped parsley and dill

Sauté the onion in oil and butter for 2 or 3 minutes, using a large skillet or heavy pot. Add the water and the cut beans and cook for about 10 minutes, covered. Add the peas, cover, and steam until barely cooked. Season, then garnish with parsley and dill. Makes 4 to 6 servings.

As mentioned before, I usually add parsley to everything I cook since, besides being nutritious, it seems to blend with all vegetables. I shall add a little celery, too, next time. And why not tomatoes? From past experience, I have also found that almost any combination of vegetables will turn into appetizing fare, especially if subtly seasoned with herbs.

To get the full benefit of garden-to-table vitamins, we have been eating beans often, cooked different ways. I try to pick beans slightly before they are mature to insure tenderness when quick-cooked. Steamed, drained, and buttered (assuming calories don't count), they are very tasty.

GREEN BEANS WITH EGGS

1 quart hot steam-cooked
  beans
2 tablespoons or less butter

2 eggs or more, beaten
salt and pepper

Drain the beans and return them to the skillet; add the butter and eggs and scramble. Season and, if available, sprinkle with chopped fresh dill fronds for a piquant flavor. This bean dish makes a big hit with guests when I serve it as a vegetable side dish, but George and I sometimes make a meal of it with fruit and maybe hot rolls. (We're perennial weight watchers.) As a vegetable course, it makes 4 to 6 servings.

GREEN BEANS WITH TOMATOES

Facilya Aboor

A good many Old Country one-dish meals combined green beans with meat, onions, and tomatoes. Served with bread in soup plates, it was simple but well-balanced fare. Sometimes I think that if we reverted to the simple one-dish meals, we would be both healthier and able to curb the overeating we are prone to in our modern civilization. Here is my modern version of this old dish.

1 quart green beans
1 chopped onion
1 tablespoon each corn oil and
  butter

½ cup water or soup stock
1½ cups canned tomatoes
salt and pepper

In a heavy pot, sauté the onion in the oil and butter for 2 or 3 minutes. Add the other ingredients, and cook until the beans are tender. Since this mixture will be soupy, serve it in individual small bowls as a side dish. Makes 4 to 6 servings.

If dill is available, chop some of the ferny fronds and add them before serving, or sprinkle them over each serving. We always have dill sticking out of various spots of the garden. Ten years ago we planted it and it has reseeded ever since. I freeze some of the early growth; then we weed it out, except in areas where it will not interfere with other plants.

The okra I planted this spring, the first time in years, added much to our bill of fare. Not usually available fresh in markets—certainly not in northern New England—it is unjustly maligned. When prepared correctly, okra is really a delicious vegetable. I learned to select and prepare it from my grandmother when we all lived in Providence, where Italian markets carried fresh okra.

OKRA WITH TOMATOES

Bamya Aboor

1 pound fresh okra	1 cup chicken broth or soup
juice of ½ lemon	stock
1 onion, slivered	1 cup canned tomatoes *or* 3 fresh
1 tablespoon each corn oil and	peeled cut-up tomatoes
butter	salt and pepper

To prepare the okra, Grandma explained as she demonstrated, the stem of each spear should be carefully cut at the seam to prevent the juices from escaping during cooking. After stemming, she put the okra in a large bowl and squeezed lemon juice over the spears early in the day. During the day, she would pick up the bowl and toss the okra periodically, to coat each spear with the lemon juice.

When it was time to cook it, she sautéed the onion in the oil and butter for 2 or 3 minutes, using a heavy cooking pot, then added the other ingredients, covered the pot, and let the okra cook until done. Makes 4 to 6 servings.

Innovations I have made include the addition of about 4 tablespoons chopped parsley and about 1 tablespoon chopped fresh basil. Who measures?

Okra freezes very well "as is." I discovered this one year when I spent several months away from home during an emergency. George was left with Dave to harvest the garden, which contained okra. They were to harvest the vegetables and handle them any way they could. They gave away most of the produce, but okra was one of Dave's favorite foods, and so he picked the spears and stuck them in the freezer, then bagged them in plastic bags. Much later, when I returned and thawed them out, I found them no different from fresh okra.

Years ago we had a large garden at the corner, some distance from our house. Once when I had planted a long row of okra, I was going to pick it but decided to wait another day. During the night a deer invaded the garden and touched nothing else but the okra, leaving a long row of stems about six inches high. It *was* a deer—we found tracks and droppings.

After Gail was born, I found it difficult with a baby to garden so far from the house and decided to plant closer, hoping to discourage deer, too. So now we get woodchucks. Guess what? I just made my daily inspection tour of the garden and found woodchuck damage again.

I walked the area and found his hole. Since it was Sunday and we were out of bombs, rather than wait until the stores opened George said he would back the pickup to the hole in the field by the garden. His plan was to attach a hose to the exhaust and put it into the hole; I was to stand by with the .22 rifle to shoot any woodchucks that tried to escape from their emergency exit, which we couldn't find to plug up.

When we finally carried out the operation no woodchucks attempted to escape. Maybe none of them were home.

I just thought of another delicious vegetable dish utilizing okra when only a few are available at a time, as happened with us this year.

MIXED STEWED VEGETABLES

Turli

Begin in the same manner as in so many of my vegetable recipes, by sautéing a large slivered onion in 2 tablespoons oil and butter. Then add a cup or 2 of chicken broth or soup stock, or water if you have neither. Add fresh peeled or canned tomatoes and a little of any or every vegetable in the garden, starting with the vegetables that take the longest to cook.

I have, at various times, combined green beans, zucchini, snow peas, carrots, broccoli, eggplant, green peppers, purslane, and Jerusalem artichokes with okra. The only vegetable I haven't used in this mixture is beets. I was afraid their deep color might give the stew a bilious appearance. I also put in herbs, such as parsley, dill, and basil. This is a great recipe for when the garden first begins to produce and you can pick only a few of each kind of vegetable.

We forced George to celebrate his birthday Monday night although he had decided to ignore it. I was going to cooperate and let it pass, since I feel exactly as he does. Who needs to be reminded after fifty? However, after we had retired the night before, Gail came in after midnight from her camp down the road and made her dad a birthday cake, decorating it with runny sentiment.

Our friend Richard Thorne, summering at their farm down the road with his wife Shirley, dropped in and discovered it was George's birthday, so stayed to celebrate. When he didn't return home, Shirley called—then decided she was going to help George celebrate too, and she walked up. We spent the night drinking to his health, whether he liked it or not, the Thornes leaving about midnight. George was trying to watch a ball game on television.

We made a healthy dent in the cake, in addition to snacking on my version of hors d'oeuvres, which included my cracker bread, always available, various cheeses, sliced turkey, sliced cucumbers, Italian olives, and a few other things I threw together in a hurry

Summer guests, a bountiful garden, and berry picking have combined to keep us continually active.

We decanted the dandelion and rhubarb wines some time ago, for final storage until Christmas. Actually, we siphoned them from one jug to another, to avoid disturbing the silt at the bottom. Using a new rubber tube from a hot water bottle combination, I started the process, but George took over when the siphoning began affecting my speech. That stuff was sure potent!

We were given a large quantity of corn last week. I talked Gail and George into making corn relish for the first time in years. George washed the pint jars, shucked and cut the corn off the cobs, and Gail did the rest of the work while I did some necessary sewing.

During a hurried shopping, I had bought red peppers to grind for the relish. It was not until Gail licked her finger after the relish was cooking that we discovered I had inadvertently bought hot red peppers instead of the sweet variety. George said he would eat the relish, and I have relatives who like hot relish.

The friend who gave us the corn told us an easy way to cut it off the cob, which George said worked fine. Using an angel cake pan, he rested the tip of each ear in the center tube hole and cut off the corn kernels, which fell off directly into the pan. We made this relish with honey, but sugar can be substituted.

HONEY CORN RELISH

10 cups corn	1½ cups honey or sugar
4 cups chopped cabbage	¼ cup pickling salt
2 cups chopped green pepper	1 tablespoon dry mustard
1 cup chopped red pepper	1 tablespoon turmeric
3 cups chopped onions	1 tablespoon celery seed
1 cup chopped celery	1 cup water
3 cups chopped unpared cucumbers	3 cups cider vinegar

Mix the vegetables in a large enamel or stainless steel pot. Add the other ingredients and bring to a boil. Simmer 5 minutes, stirring occasionally. Fill the hot pint jars to the brim and seal them immediately. Makes 10 pints.

I run a butter knife around the jars to dispel the air bubbles, then press down with a teaspoon to bring the liquid to the brim. Use one small hot pepper for zing. (We used six!) Grind all the vegetables through the coarse blade of a food chopper.

While storing the corn relish, I noticed that our supply of pickles and relishes was almost gone, and there was only one pint jar of my green tomato mincemeat left. I picked a cool day to start replenishing the cellar larder.

GREEN TOMATO MINCEMEAT

This recipe, undoubtedly a prizewinner, was given to me by a dear old lady who farmed with her elderly brother where the Thornes now live during the summers. Both she and her brother have long since gone to their reward.

6 quarts ground green tomatoes	2 cups cider vinegar
6 pints ground unpared apples	2 tablespoons cinnamon
6 pounds brown sugar	1 tablespoon ground cloves
2 pounds seedless raisins	1 tablespoon allspice
1 pound corn oil margarine	2 teaspoons salt

Cover the tomatoes with water, bring to a boil, and strain. Discard the water. Repeat. In a large enamel or stainless steel pot, combine all the ingredients, bring to a boil, and simmer about 30 minutes. Fill hot pint jars to the brim and seal. Makes about 17 pints. One pint will be enough for an 8-inch pie. The original recipe called for 2 cups of suet instead of the margarine.

Here are other favorite pickle and relish recipes I have gleaned from old-timers in the area, most of them now gone:

BREAD AND BUTTER PICKLES

3 quarts sliced cucumbers	1 teaspoon cinnamon
3 sliced onions	1 teaspoon turmeric
½ cup pickling salt	½ teaspoon ginger
3 cups cider vinegar	½ teaspoon celery seed
1 cup water	2 tablespoons mustard seed
1½ cups brown sugar	1 pod hot pepper (optional)

Combine the cucumbers, onions, and salt, and let stand 5 hours. In a large enamel or stainless steel pot, combine the other ingredients and bring to a boil. Drain the vegetables, then add them to the hot liquid, boil 1 minute, and pack into hot pint jars. Seal immediately. Makes about 6 pints.

PICCALILLI

7 pounds green tomatoes	1 cup brown sugar
3 green peppers	2 tablespoons mustard seed
1 head cabbage	1 tablespoon celery seed
2 large onions	1 quart cider vinegar
½ cup pickling salt	

Chop and mix all the vegetables. Add the salt and let stand overnight. Combine the other ingredients in a large enamel or stainless steel pot, and stir and boil for 1 minute. Drain the vegetables, add them to the pot, bring to a boil, and simmer 5 minutes. Pack hot pint jars to the brim and seal at once. Makes about 9 pints.

ZINGY GREEN TOMATO AND APPLE RELISH

6 pounds green tomatoes	3 tablespoons pickling salt
8 tart red apples	1 tablespoon cinnamon
6 sweet red peppers	1½ teaspoons ground cloves
8 onions	5 cups sugar
1 small hot pepper	1 quart cider vinegar

Core the apples but do not pare them. Put the vegetables and apples through the coarse blade of the food chopper. Combine the other ingredients in a large enamel or stainless steel pot, and bring to the boil. Add the vegetables and apples and simmer 20 minutes, stirring occasionally. Pack to the brim in hot pint jars and seal.

When putting vegetables and apples through the food chopper, I spread newspaper on the floor and set a glass bowl under the chopper, to catch the juices. I return all juices to the mixture except the green tomato juice, which I discard to prevent the relish from being too soupy. Substitute sweet green peppers if you can't find red peppers. Works fine.

GOLDEN RELISH

I make this relish with the huge overripe cucumbers that were overlooked during other pickings. It is a bit of work because the vegetables have to be diced, but so good it's worth the trouble.

12 large cucumbers	6 sweet red peppers
12 onions	1 quart cider vinegar
¾ cup pickling salt	4 cups sugar
2 large bunches celery	2 tablespoons mustard seed

Peel the cucumbers, scoop out and discard the seeds. Dice cucumbers and onions in cubes and mix with the salt. Let stand overnight. Drain well, and add the diced celery and peppers. Combine the other ingredients in a large enamel or stainless steel kettle, add the vegetables, bring to a boil, and simmer until thick and the cucumbers are golden. Pack in hot jars and seal at once. Makes about 6 pints.

GARLIC DILL PICKLES

Wash the cucumbers. Leave the small ones whole, but slice the large ones lengthwise in four pieces and bottle them separately. Into each quart jar, put 1 large clove of garlic, 1 grape leaf (optional, if you can't find any), 2 heads of dill, and 1 small hot pepper for zing, if desired. Then pack in the cucumbers and top each jar with ⅛ teaspoon of alum.

In a large enamel or stainless steel pot, combine 1 quart cider vinegar, 3 quarts water, and 1 cup pickling salt. Heat to boiling, fill the packed jars to the brim, and seal at once. Makes about 8 quarts.

I put the jars on the stove near the pot to keep them warm enough so that they don't break when I pour in the vinegar mixture.

Mosquitoes nearly finished me off one hot day when a fun trip to identify and gather edible wild plants—later to eat them for lunch—turned into a nightmare.

I joined nine youths, a young couple and their two sons, and our teacher and guide on the venture. The couple and their children dropped out a quarter of the way through and I gave up a little more than halfway through.

Anticipating mosquitoes, I arose early to make myself a pair of cool slacks out of some old lightweight draperies, since I'd rather suffer from heat than from mosquitoes or blackflies. My one mistake in judgment was to wear a short-sleeved shirt. I cut up a nylon curtain and draped it around my Chico Marx Italian straw to protect my face and neck, grabbed my plastic bucket and some insect repellent, and took off.

We were to meet at 10 A.M. at the mouth of a dirt road crudely hacked out of the wilderness. Our guide and expert on edible plants, a young girl who lived deep in the woods, met us and gave us a short introductory lecture. We started our trip by identifying such plants as sheep sorrel, wild mustard, sedum, and Japanese knotweed by the road, and gathered some for lunch. The insect attack began when we started down the dirt road into the woods. The deeper we went in, the more we swatted. When we reached a bog area, the mosquito hum sounded like the drone of a plane. The couple and their youngsters gave up the fight at the bog, mostly for the sake of the children. I almost returned with them, but didn't want to call attention to my age by chickening out. Instead, I swabbed my arms again with repellent gunk and pressed on.

Our destination, the woodland home of our guide, was a mile in, I learned, and secretly wondered if I could walk it. However, counting the side trips—one to gather watercress from a clear brook, where we also quenched our thirst—we must have walked much more than a mile. I passed up the last side trip and decided to go on alone the rest of the way to the crude house, stumbling ahead in a state of delirium, a cloud of humming mosquitoes around my netted head. The door was opened by a young girl and I dashed in along with about sixty mosquitoes. They joined many others buzzing merrily in the room. The young girl said her name was Amy.

"Don't these mosquitoes bother you?" I asked incredulously, as she calmly brushed them aside by waving her hand across her face. I noticed she had been making a buttercup chain on one of the raised wooden-slab beds, the only furniture in the room.

"Not really—I guess I'm used to them," she replied.

I dropped my hot, weary body on one of the beds. Amy offered me water from a glass jug on the floor and I accepted gratefully. After that I kept up a steady swat until the group came, laden with plants and bringing in more mosquitoes. The prospect of swatting mosquitoes throughout the cleaning, scraping, and cooking of the plants, and then trying to eat, was too much for me. Even a promised dessert of Japanese knotweed pie failed to entice me. I left as gracefully as I could, after donning my hat and veil and picking up my empty bucket. I hadn't taken enough time off from swatting to gather any plants.

Flailing my arms the entire time, I puffed back to my car, done in by the three miles I had walked. Some time later, I concluded such discomforts help a person to appreciate simple blessings like a bath, iced tea, and a screened porch.

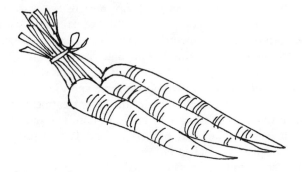

September

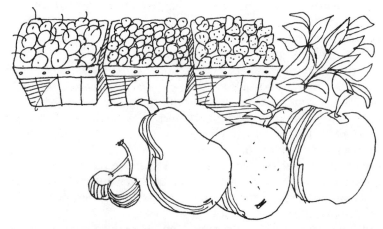

URING September, we heedfully listen to weather reports so that the first killing frost will not come as a surprise. When the weatherman forecasts frost, we pick all the tomatoes, cucumbers, melons, zucchini and other squash, and peppers. Taking our supply of bushel baskets into the garden, we start with the tomatoes. Actually, we pick into light plastic pails, and separate the tomatoes into the baskets according to their degree of ripeness—very green, beginning to turn, almost ripe, and ripe.

A certain number of cucumbers and zucchini we keep in our refrigerators for eating, and we pickle some and give some to neighbors and friends. The cantaloupes get the same treatment, but instead of pickling them, I cut a few into cubes to combine and freeze with other fruit, such as our peaches, pears, and late raspberries. (Our variety of raspberry yields a fall crop, too.)

The butternut squash goes in the barn until it hardens, if it has not already done so on the vines. During very cold nights, we throw old blankets over the pile. Later we store them in a cool (50° to 60°) dry place. The best place here, we discovered one winter, is Gail's bedroom; we shut off the heat and spread the squash over an old blanket on the floor. Squash should be picked with their stems and handled carefully, to prevent scrapes or scratches that would cause decay. Our stored supply in Gail's room lasted until April.

Pepper plants are hung upside down in the unheated utility room, peppers and all. The peppers keep for weeks—if not eaten.

We eat our root crops before they need to be stored. However, years ago when the whole family was home and we had a larger garden, we stored carrots, beets, potatoes, and cabbage in the cellar. These crops must be kept cold and they need an area with some moisture. Last winter I successfully stored Jerusalem artichokes in damp sand until spring when they were still crisp and delicious. Carrots and beets could probably be stored the same way.

I usually pot some herbs and place them on the sunny porch for winter use. Others, such as sage, marjoram, and mint, I tie in bunches and hang upside down, strung across the sunniest end of the porch.

Tomato canning starts after the killing frost at our house. George usually prepares the jars and peels the tomatoes, and I bottle and process them when I get home. The smallest green tomatoes are kept separate for use in relishes, pickles, and green tomato mincemeat.

I plant chard instead of spinach because it can be cut often and grows again. Besides, it is hardy and does not freeze in the garden, but keeps us supplied with greens until the snows come. I also freeze some for winter use.

I never freeze vegetables or fruit according to the prescribed methods. I stopped blanching years ago, since it seemed to me that vitamins were lost in the process. I steam greens until they wilt, and heat other vegetables through, using as little water as possible, covering the utensil, a heavy stainless steel pot, and stirring frequently for a few minutes. Most of the water evaporates. After steaming, I spread the vegetables one layer deep on trays, which I set on trivets to cool as quickly as possible with the help of the air circulation underneath, before they are packaged and frozen.

To freeze fruit from our peach, plum, and pear trees, I slice it into containers, add honey, and meld together, sometimes combining several fruits. I run to the freezer with each package to keep the fruit from discoloring. Only the peaches are skinned—by immersing them in hot water for about one minute. One day I washed and cut up unpeeled pears into pint plastic containers, added pineapple juice, and stuck the containers in the freezer. I shall add a pint of these to other fruits in the winter when I make fruit cocktail.

Elderberries, blueberries, blackberries, and raspberries are frozen dry without any treatment except to pick them over. When my children were young, they restored frozen berries to their fresh flavor by combining them with cold cereal and pouring hot milk over all, thawing the berries instantly. Although small strawberries are frozen in the same manner as the berries mentioned above, I slice or halve large ones before putting them in containers to meld with a little honey.

In addition to putting them in fruit cocktail, during the winter months I use frozen and bottled fruits to make pies, puddings, jams, and other desserts. Sometimes we just eat partially thawed fruit or berries.

I can tell fall is definitely here by looking at the swale as I sit on the porch. We had a row of elm trees between the lawn and the swale, but they all died from Dutch elm disease so Babe cut them down, also clearing part of the swale behind the grapevines on the stone wall. Now that area is a rhapsody in blue with various kinds of wild asters, from a pale shade to indigo, a lovely contrast against the still green shrubs. Ah, me—if fall is here, can winter be far behind? Yuk!

I took a walk to pick a winter bouquet for the porch and returned with two varieties of grass and sprigs of tiny, hardly visible bell-shaped flowers. Being colorblind, I'm not sure of the color—I think, very pale blue. It is too early for most winter bouquet material. I found the grasses and flowers by the side of the road. Later, there will be milkweed pods and red berries on a type of bush I have yet to identify. I wish I could find out if they were edible or suitable for jams and jellies.

When I picked some wild grapes in a field across from our place, I found an empty bird's nest among the vines. Nostalgia engulfed me as I remembered all the times I had helped my sons retrieve such nests for their collection. I can't remember what eventually happened to all the nests but while Babe and Dave were collecting them, we displayed them on the barn crosspieces between the studs. Once when Babe was seven, he tried to shoot down an empty oriole's nest hanging from the end of a limb on the huge stately elm in front of our house (another victim of Dutch elm disease) with his bow and arrow. To his surprise, the arrow pierced the nest and both stayed on the tree until the next spring. Well, there I go, off on a tangent again ...

I also went to our corner field to pick the grapes on our stone wall there, and en route I discovered and grieved over the collapse of our old Baldwin apple tree. Although the huge tree was split and had been partially hollowed out and infirm for years, it bravely continued to bear apples. When all our other old apple trees were cut down more than twenty years ago, I insisted on keeping the Baldwin tree. I like to think it repaid me by continuing to bear. I patted the fallen piece of trunk and said, "Well done, thou good and faithful servant," then went home with my pail full of grapes. Luckily, no one was around to hear me.

Gail asked for a shish-kebab cookout before returning to school, so we had one. This is the perfect time of year for such a cookout, as garden tomatoes and green peppers are available to string on the shish, or skewer. The other requirement is a sunny fall day and, in our case, the weather cooperated.

SHISH KEBAB

Cut up the lean portion of a leg of lamb into small chunks a little larger than a walnut. Use only well-trimmed, solid pieces of meat. Sprinkle these generously with meat tenderizer, and add 1 chopped onion, 1 large clove chopped garlic, ¼ cup corn oil, and salt and pepper to taste. Mix these ingredients well with the meat chunks, and marinate in a covered bowl in the refrigerator for several hours, preferably overnight.

Get someone to make a charcoal fire in the grill outside. At our house, this is George's job. We prefer the real charcoal, not the ersatz chemicalized briquets.

Cut medium tomatoes in quarters, then eighths; or use whole cherry tomatoes. Cut the peppers in squares. Prepare the long skewers by inserting them into a piece of meat, a chunk of tomato, another piece of meat, a piece of pepper, then meat, and so on up the skewer, ending with meat. Begin the broiling when the fire has died down to red coals.

Lamb is the traditional meat for shish kebab, but I see no reason why lean tender beef should not be used if more readily available. Someday I shall try a mixture of lamb and beef.

Vegetables may be omitted on the skewers. If only meat is used, put the chunks on without crowding so that they will cook evenly. I serve this superb meat dish with rice pilav and baked eggplant.

When a spell of hot weather finally cooled off, I made braised lamb and bulgur pilav for George. I like it too, but seldom remember to make it until I get a subtle suggestion from him, such as "When are you going to make lamb and pilav again?"

With meat prices skyrocketing, I have been buying New Zealand lamb and find it excellent meat—really tender lamb. I suspect some of the domestic lamb I bought in the past was yearling. The legs were tougher and larger.

To make braised lamb, I usually use neck slices and shanks, which around here are packaged together and more reasonably priced than other cuts. However, shoulder lamb chops can also be used by themselves or mixed with the neck slices and shanks.

BRAISED LAMB

Put the lamb pieces in a heavy skillet, and add about ¼ cup water and 1 teaspoon salt, depending on the quantity of lamb. Cover, bring to a boil, and simmer until the lamb is tender. Uncover, and simmer until all water has evaporated. Some fat should be rendered from the meat; if it is too lean, add 1 or 2 tablespoons of oil and let the meat brown over low heat for about 20 minutes, stirring frequently. Serve with rice, grains, vegetables, noodles, mashed potatoes—or anything else, for that matter, that you like.

LAMB-WHEAT STEW

Here is a really superb lamb stew for the cold weather. I make it with lamb neck slices but sliced lamb shanks and shoulder chops would be suitable, too. Do try it.

6 cups water
1½ pounds lamb neck or shank
  slices
1 teaspoon salt
½ cup hulled wheat
2 cups coarsely chopped onions
1 cup diced turnip

¼ cup fresh minced parsley *or*
  1 tablespoon dry parsley flakes
1 clove garlic, minced, *or*
  ⅛ teaspoon garlic powder
¼ teaspoon powdered mace
black pepper to taste

Bring the water to a boil in a large heavy pot with cover. Add the meat, salt, and wheat, and simmer for about 1½ hours. Add the vegetables, parsley, garlic, mace, and black pepper, preferably fresh ground. Simmer about 20 minutes more and serve. Makes about 6 servings. Accompanied by garlic bread and fruit, it is a balanced meal. Make a green salad if more vegetables are desired.

Someone once offered us a pet goat named William. Since it was free and didn't need milking, I accepted. William had the run of the farm like Wiggy, our part-collie and part-Dalmatian dog. The two played and roamed around together. Both of them accompanied us on blueberrying trips in our pasture and generally followed us during walks.

William got bolder each year and began getting on my nerves. He was a very dumb goat and much harder to control than Wiggy, who was a highly intelligent dog. One summer day when my mother was visiting, she decided to take an afternoon nap in the boys' tent under the maple tree. The tent was furnished with a double bed spring and mattress, and the boys slept there during the summer.

While my mother napped, William sashayed in through the flap, walked right over her and out through the slit in the back end. By that act, he sacrificed his precarious position and sealed his doom. William was dressed off and, disguised as a lamb, fed to a bunch of fraternity boys from Brown University, who complimented the cook after the meal. My mother was the cook.

Recently, when guests were expected, I made a meat loaf that was really superior and full of extra nutrition, too. Instead of using bread to keep the loaf tender, I used wheat germ—without divulging the innovation, of course. Everyone said it was great.

MEAT LOAF WITH WHEAT GERM

2 pounds ground chuck or part ground pork	salt and pepper
1 cup wheat germ	½ teaspoon sage
1 large onion, chopped	½ teaspoon poultry seasoning
1 or 2 eggs	1 teaspoon curry powder
½ cup chopped parsley	½ teaspoon basil
1 small green pepper, chopped	1 large clove garlic, minced
	1 cup canned tomatoes

If the meat is too lean, add a little corn oil. Combine all the ingredients thoroughly, then shape in a long loaf, set on a trivet in a baking pan, and brush the loaf with oil. Bake about one hour in a 350° oven. My meat loaves come out different each time I make one, depending on the ingredients I have available. Recently, for maximum protein, I have also been adding mashed cooked soybeans to the mixture since I discovered the value of this bean. I experiment with spices, too.

Sometimes I add dry mustard to the mixture. Meat loaf is a fine food for creative expression. Here is another one:

JUICY SPICED MEAT PATTIES

1 pound ground beef or lamb, or mixture of both
1 onion, chopped
1 egg
1 clove garlic, minced
1 small green pepper, chopped
2 tablespoons corn oil

2 or 3 tablespoons chopped parsley
½ to 1 cup mashed cooked soybeans
½ teaspoon curry powder
½ teaspoon sage
½ cup bread crumbs (preferably whole wheat) or wheat germ

Combine all the ingredients well with the hands. The amount of oil depends on how lean the meat is. If the mixture is too dry, add a little milk. The spices are a matter of taste and may be omitted. Shape into patties and broil.

Here is a meat dish cooked by my sister, Rose, affectionately known as Pook (rhymes with book), who came to visit us from California during this month. It is easy to make and very tasty, but I made some changes in keeping with my desire to eat pure unadulterated foods.

GROUND BEEF STROGANOFF

1 pound ground lean chuck
1 onion, chopped
1 clove garlic, minced
1 tablespoon corn oil
2 tablespoons flour

1 cup fresh sliced mushrooms or canned mushrooms
salt and pepper to taste
1 can cream of chicken soup
1 cup sour cream

Sauté the onion and garlic in oil 2 or 3 minutes, add meat, and brown. Stir in the flour, mushrooms, salt and pepper to taste, and cook 10 minutes. Add the soup and cook 5 minutes; then add the sour cream and heat through. Serve over cooked egg noodles, rice, or mashed potatoes.

Instead of canned soup, I used chicken broth and 4 tablespoons flour for thickening, and seasoned with my flavor salt. I beat 1 cup of plain yogurt with an egg and substituted this for the sour cream.

A close friend who is very aware of good nutrition was married in a lovely outdoor wedding on a cool, sunny September day. She lives on a farm in the same town we do. The barn next to her house was cleaned, decorated in a fall motif, and used for the reception refreshments. Wooden tables were loaded with many kinds of stone-ground whole wheat breads, cakes, and muffins, several wheels of cheeses, cheese spreads, almonds, cashews, pumpkin seeds, sunflower seeds, and bowls of fruit. There were fresh-pressed cider and coffee to drink.

Recognizing beforehand that here would be a perfect opportunity to try a health recipe without having to eat it all myself (you know George!), I made a bulgur salad and took it with us in a large wooden bowl. I gave it to the bride's mother, with three golden tomatoes that I had snatched up from the kitchen at the last moment, to slice over the salad. These tomatoes were a new variety from two plants given to me.

There were many interesting nonestablishment people there, and I milled around thoroughly enjoying the scene, being a little off-center myself. I talked so much that by the time I got to the salad to give George a taste, a hippie guest was scraping the bowl with a piece of bread. But I did plenty of tasting when I made it.

BULGUR SALAD

2 cups coarse bulgur
1 quart boiling water
1 teaspoon salt (about)
½ cup olive or corn oil
1 cup chopped scallions or
   onions
1 large cucumber, thinly sliced
⅓ cup lemon juice

1 cup chopped parsley
¼ cup chopped mixed dill
   fronds and mint leaves
1 green pepper, chopped
2 cloves garlic, minced
4 ears fresh corn (optional)
salt and pepper

Combine the bulgur, salt, and water in a heavy pot with a tight cover and simmer about 20 minutes until the bulgur is cooked and the water absorbed. Remove the cover and allow to cool completely.

Transfer to a large bowl, add the other ingredients, and mix thoroughly, separating the kernels of bulgur. Serve on crisp lettuce or romaine, if desired. If corn is used, steam it covered for about 5 minutes, cut the kernels off the cobs, and cool before adding to the salad.

The quantities listed will make too much salad for a small family. Halve all ingredients and, if it is still too much, serve it to guests.

October

IT IS ALMOST dusk on a mild October afternoon. I am on the glassed-in porch watching a phoebe bathing in the birdbath under the crab apple tree while a meadow lark keeps flitting by, awaiting his turn. The birdbath, a birthday gift to George from Babe and Judy, gives us as much pleasure as it does the birds. Babe installed it in a perfect location, in a clearing between the porch and the woodsy swale.

These calm Indian summer afternoons are so colorful and poignant. I am trying to analyze why I feel sad as I listen to the chirping crickets. Probably because the lush vegetation will soon disappear under the snow, leaving only the evergreens and the stark bare branches of the other trees. I still prefer spring and the rebirth of nature, heralded by the mating songs of birds, which we later watch building their nests, many in the same spots year after year.

Gail has returned to school, and the two of us are preparing for the winter. We have cleaned up most of the garden and are now storing the stakes used to hold up the branches of our dwarf fruit trees, when they are heavily laden with fruit. We take this precaution because we lost several branches that broke from the weight of the fruit. We find dwarf and semi-dwarf trees prolific and easy to manage and pick.

Our quince tree bore for the first time this year, five perfect quinces! I was enchanted, since I have been unable to buy this fruit

123

around here. Quince preserves, in my opinion, are in a class by themselves, fragrant and unique. I shall slice and stew my precious harvest with honey.

I almost lost the filbert tree harvest this year. The small tree bore a few nuts for the first time last year, and I knew nuts had formed under some of the leaves this year. A few days ago when I remembered to check again, I found only hulls. Examining the ground underneath, where the grass had grown quite tall, I found a couple of the nuts. When I searched the area carefully, getting down on my hands and knees and feeling the ground for lumps, they invariably turned out to be nuts. The total harvest was 9 nuts, which I cracked and ate myself.

As a side dish for Sunday dinner, I cooked one of our butternut squashes and gave my portion a gourmet touch by adding a few shelled hickory nuts. Delicious! George, as I've said, is something of a hash-house eater—he prefers most foods without embellishment and especially objects to nuts.

Try this mashed squash recipe on anyone who claims he does not like squash. I can almost guarantee you will convert him.

MASHED SQUASH WITH HONEY

1 medium butternut squash or other winter squash	¼ cup honey
½ cup water	⅛ teaspoon ground cardamon seed
salt	pepper, freshly ground
1 to 2 tablespoons butter	½ cup broken nuts (optional)

Peel the squash, cut it into cubes, and put in a saucepan. Add water and some salt, cover, and cook it until soft. Drain, mash, then add butter, honey, and cardamon, if available. Add pepper, preferably freshly ground, and fold in the nutmeats (if used).

Here are two more dandy squash recipes.

SQUASH WITH PRUNES AND NUTS

3 cups mashed squash	5 to 10 prunes (or dates) cut in bits
¼ teaspoon salt	¼ to ½ cup chopped nuts
¼ cup honey or sugar	
¼ teaspoon cardamon or other preferred spice	

Combine all the ingredients and bake in a covered casserole at 350° about 30 minutes. If squash is too dry, add a little orange juice or other fruit juice. Any winter squash can be used in this recipe.

I sprung this squash dish as a surprise to George. When he opened the casserole and saw the dark bits of prunes he asked, "What happened to your squash? Did it stick to the bottom and burn?"

"No, dear," I replied icily, "you just don't recognize a gourmet dish when you see one." Imagine!

BAKED BUTTERNUT SQUASH WITH HONEY

Split 1 or 2 butternut squash through the center lengthwise and scoop out the seeds with a small spoon. Place the halves on a baking pan. Put a lump of butter and a tablespoon or two of honey in each cavity, and sprinkle the halves with salt and pepper. Cover the bottom of the baking pan with ½ inch of water and bake the squash at 350° until soft. We each eat half a squash by spooning pulp from around the sides and dipping each spoonful into the honey-butter mixture in the center of the cavity.

During a hungry moment recently, I discovered that raw butternut squash is delicious too. George had peeled and cubed one ready for me to cook. I was so ravenous when I got home, I started gnawing on a cube as I added water to the pan for cooking.

I should explain here that I fast periodically to rest my overworked digestive system and, hopefully, lose some weight. When I ate the raw squash, I was breaking a two-day fast. I don't guarantee the same fine flavor from a store-bought squash. In the past I have found that it does not measure up to the homegrown butternut in flavor. Anyhow, I slivered some into my salad later.

Apple season is always a vividly hued time of year with goldenrod and purple asters in bloom, contrasting with the red woodbine climbing over gray stone walls and tree trunks by our road.

I walked to our corner field and then to the Thornes' old apple orchard to check apple drops. With their permission, we have been taking the drops to Hillside Orchards for the past two years, where Ozzie transforms every 6 bushels into about 18 gallons of cider. We have been collecting jugs with rubberized tops for cider storage. When George returns with the cider, I bring it to a boil in my large cauldrons, skim the top foam, and pour the cider into canning jars or any jars with rubberized covers. George tightens the screwtop seals immediately for a vacuum pack. The cider or apple juice stays sweet until we open the bottle again.

When we ran short of bottles one year, young friends in the "aware" group told us we could get a vacuum seal with screw tops having cardboard inserts. We tried them and found they worked. Cider pressed fresh at local orchards does not have questionable food additives and remains fresh apple juice if immediately bottled by this method.

Cider freezes in a unique pattern, probably as a result of the same principle that causes it, when fermented, to turn into high-proof applejack. The sugar content concentrates in the core, leaving a bland-flavored rim. I freeze some in small plastic containers, and when Gail is home, we hack at the frozen contents with a spoon as we read.

Here are a fine cake and icing, both made with fresh cider.

APPLE JUICE CAKE

½ cup or 1 stick corn oil margarine	½ teaspoon salt
	½ teaspoon cinnamon
1 cup or a little less sugar	½ teaspoon nutmeg
2 eggs	¼ teaspoon cloves
2 cups flour	¾ cup apple juice
1 teaspoon baking powder	½ teaspoon vanilla
½ teaspoon baking soda	

Cream the margarine and sugar until light and fluffy. Add the eggs one at a time, beating well after each addition. Sift or stir together the dry ingredients and spices. Add these to the creamed mixture in three portions, alternately with the apple juice in two portions. Add vanilla. Bake in two 8 inch round layer pans at 375° for 25 to 30 minutes. One-half cup raisins can be added to the batter with the vanilla and part of the sugar replaced with honey if desired.

FLUFFY APPLE JUICE ICING

1 cup sugar	1 tablespoon lemon juice
½ cup apple juice	2 egg whites
pinch of salt	

Combine all the ingredients except the egg whites in a saucepan, and cook until the syrup forms a soft ball (234° to 240°) when a little is dropped into a cup of ice water. Pour the syrup slowly over the stiffly beaten egg whites, beating constantly until the mixture stands in soft peaks. Spread the icing between the layers and on the top and sides of the cake. Nuts or coconut may be sprinkled over the icing.

Since this is the time to cook with apples and cider, here are more of our favorite recipes.

DUTCH APPLE CAKE

1½ cups flour	1 egg
1 tablespoon baking powder	⅔ cup milk
½ teaspoon salt	4 or 5 tart apples
2 tablespoons sugar	½ cup sugar (about)
4 tablespoons butter or corn oil margarine	½ teaspoon pumpkin pie spice

Combine the first four ingredients and cut in the butter or margarine. Beat the egg and milk together and add to the dry ingredients to make a soft dough. Spread the dough in the bottom of an 8 x 12 inch or similar-size pan, brush with soft butter or oil, and cover with thinly sliced apples arranged in parallel rows. Sprinkle with the ½ cup of sugar and the spice, and bake at 375° about 25 minutes. Embellish any way desired when serving.

APPLE-HONEY PUDDING

5 or 6 tart apples	1 egg
¼ cup honey	½ cup honey (about)
1 cup flour preferably whole wheat	¼ cup cider or water
1 teaspoon baking powder	2 tablespoons corn oil
pinch of salt	1 teaspoon cinnamon
	1 teaspoon nutmeg

Slice the apples and arrange them in an 8 x 12 inch baking pan. Drizzle the ¼ cup honey over them. Combine the flour, baking powder, salt, egg, and the ½ cup honey into a batter, and distribute it over the apples. Combine the cider or water and oil, and sprinkle it over the batter, then sprinkle spices on top and bake at 350° 30 to 40 minutes. Serve with ice cream, plain yogurt, or sour cream, if desired.

APPLE-BREAD PUDDING

I tried this pudding one day recently when I found a forgotten loaf of my stone-ground whole wheat bread in the freezer the day before we were expecting Babe and Judy to visit. I thawed it out and used it for the base of the pudding.

8 slices of stale or toasted bread	½ cup honey, sugar, or
½ cup raisins	maple syrup
4 or 5 tart apples, sliced	1 to 2 teaspoons pumpkin pie
3 cups scalded milk	spice
2 tablespoons corn oil or butter	⅛ teaspoon salt

4 large eggs

Butter or oil an 8 x 12 inch pan and line it with the bread cut in cubes. Sprinkle on and tuck in the raisins and the thinly sliced apples. Combine the other ingredients, except the eggs, with the scalded milk, and pour them over the bread. Let stand a few minutes. Beat the eggs and pour over all. Bake at 350° until the custardy mixture is set— maybe 50 minutes, I don't remember. This pudding is not very sweet. More syrup or honey may be added at serving time, or a dollop of sweetened whipped cream for the lucky skinny people.

If George liked nuts (outside of me, of course), I would have put a handful of hickory or cashew nuts in the pudding.

APPLE-COTTAGE CHEESE SALAD

This is one of my favorite salads, especially in winter. I often make a meal of it. Others to whom I have served it always ask for the recipe.

4 tart apples, diced	1 tablespoon honey
½ cup raisins	1 tablespoon lemon juice
½ cup chopped nuts	⅛ teaspoon salt

Toss all the ingredients with a dressing made by combining ¼ cup cottage cheese, ¼ cup of plain yogurt or sour cream, and a little salt.

BAKED STUFFED APPLES

Ozzie gave me some huge apples, which he called 20-ounce Pippins, with instructions to try them baked. I sneakily ate one raw, but baked the other four. They were great!

Without paring them, I cored them not quite through to the blossom end, filled the holes with honey, inserted a pitted date in each, and sprinkled them with my spice mixture similar to pumpkin pie spice. I forgot to add some nuts. By now, everyone must suspect that I am mad about nuts. When serving the apples, I thought of adding a dollop of ice cream or yogurt, but talked myself out of it to keep the calories down. Try stuffing apples with raisins if dates are not immediately available.

Here is one of the few cakes I have been able to make using only stone-ground whole wheat flour that came out tender, light, and delicious. Gail made one originally with applesauce and without eggs. I revised the recipe, using two large eggs and our own red plums, some of which I had bottled because there was no more room in our freezers last year when we had a bumper crop.

I used no sugar or other sweetening agents when I bottled the plums. I think any fruit can be used in this cake, but be sure to cut down the amount of sugar or honey if the fruit has been sweetened. The applesauce Gail used I had bottled from our McIntosh apple tree, again without sugar. The apples were very ripe at the time and unusually sweet. Anyhow, both cakes were excellent.

PLUM OR APPLESAUCE CAKE

3 cups whole wheat flour
1 teaspoon cinnamon
1 teaspoon cloves
2 teaspoons baking soda
2 eggs (optional)
½ cup corn oil

2 cups applesauce, plum, or other fruit pulp
1½ cups or less sugar or part honey
1 to 2 cups raisins and/or nuts

Combine the flour, spices, and soda, and put aside. Separate the eggs and beat the whites until peaks form. Beat the egg yolks, oil, applesauce or pulp, and sugar in a mixing bowl, add the flour mixture, and fold in the egg whites, raisins, and nuts. Bake in rectangular pan, about 13 X 9 inches with 2-inch sides, for 45 to 55 minutes at 350°.

A heaping tablespoon of powdered milk and/or soya powder can also be included with the dry ingredients. Personally, I put the raisins in the cake and sprinkle the chopped nuts thickly on top of the batter before baking. This is a large cake, suitable for entertaining. Cut the ingredients in half for a small family, and bake about 35 minutes.

Most young homemakers will not remember the open bins of dried apples sold in country stores long ago. When I was a little girl, I would nag my mother to buy some every time we went to a certain store. I was mad about dried apples, especially for winter nibbling. Last year I started making my own, and discovered I'm still mad about dried apples.

DRIED APPLES

Peel and core tart apples and slice them in thin rounds. I use Baldwins. Place the slices on trays in one layer, and dry them in a 110°-to-150° oven for 4 to 6 hours. The fruit should feel dry outside and slightly soft inside. Store in a glass container, stirring occasionally the first few days to distribute any moisture evenly.

Babe and Judy visited us with a big shopping bag full of quince last weekend. Babe knows I prize quince for its superb flavor in jam and when stewed. The quince, that is. He also knows I can't find any around.

Anyhow, he and Judy recently moved into a historic neighborhood in Rehoboth, Massachusetts, and being an extremely observant person, he noticed some quince trees in the vicinity as be began commuting to his teaching post in Providence. He told me that he finally stopped at one house and asked the lady of the house if she used the quince. When she told him she didn't, he asked if she minded if he picked some.

"No—take all you want," she said. "It will save me from raking them up all over the lawn. The children throw them at each other."

Encouraged by her generosity, after picking a shopping bag almost full, he approached another house where there were several trees loaded with ripe fruit. He asked the woman there if he could pick the fruit, and she kept repeating, "They're better off on the tree!" There was an empty house next door with more loaded quince trees, so Babe asked the woman if she knew who owned that property. She replied, "They're better off on the tree!" He said he left after that, as he felt there was no point in pursuing the subject.

I was happy to get the one bag of quince, and I made both quince jam and quince butter.

QUINCE JAM

I can't remember how many quinces I washed, cored, and sliced into a large pot, but after barely covering them with water and cooking for 20 minutes, I had 5 cups of the fruit and liquid. I dumped the measured fruit into a large, heavy stainless steel pot, added 4 cups of sugar, and boiled the mixture to the jelling stage, then poured it in glasses and topped them with paraffin.

The quinces Babe brought were quite sour and not fancy and as sweet as the few from our new tree. If we ever get enough from our tree for jam, I think I shall add some lemon juice to the mixture, too. I think the batch I made would fill about 11 regular glasses. I can't be sure, since I'm down to using odds and ends of jars.

QUINCE BUTTER

Core the fruit, cut it in slices, barely cover them with water, and simmer until soft. Put the fruit through a food mill and measure it. Add ½ as much sugar and a few grains of salt. Bring the mixture to a boil, stir frequently and simmer uncovered until thick, up to 2 hours or more. Use a heavy pot and stir often to keep the thick mixture from sticking. While it is cooking, add cinnamon, cloves, and allspice if desired.

The butter is done if no rim of liquid separates when a spoonful is dropped on a cold surface. Fill hot pint jars to the brim and seal immediately. Apple butter can be made in the same manner.

Taking a now-seldom-used road to work recently, I passed the deserted North Road Community Club and remembered the good times we had there years ago. The club members held weekly square and round dancing with a live orchestra. By virtue of buying one of the farms formerly owned by a charter member, we automatically became members.

I was first introduced to square dancing there, and never ceased to wonder at the stamina of many old-timers, who lasted through the whole evening of dancing, mostly square dancing. Although I was in my prime then, I had all I could do to keep going through one square dance.

Most of the members were farmers, and one night I overheard one wondering over the growing manure pile outside another farmer's leaning barn. "Heck," said his neighbor, "he don't dare spread that manure—it's the only thing holding the barn up!"

The old crowd is gone now, and so are most of the farms. Summer people are occupying many of them and farming here has petered out, mostly, I think, because farmers worked too hard for the little money they made. I can vouch for that, since we tried it on a small scale. I still remember my backache after picking a rounded bushel of green beans from our corner garden to sell for two dollars. Once was enough.

We often had community dinners there for which each family took a casserole, salad, rolls, or some other food. A salad we first ate there is still a family favorite. It is attractive, simple to make, and a fine accompaniment to poultry.

CRANBERRY-COTTAGE CHEESE SALAD

1 pound cottage cheese	salt and pepper
chopped chives or onions	1 can whole berry cranberry
½ cup plain yogurt or sour	sauce
cream	chopped nuts (optional)
lettuce	

Combine the cheese, chives or onions to taste, yogurt or sour cream, and seasoning. Spoon the mixture and the cranberry sauce separately on lettuce cups. Arrange alternately on a platter. Sprinkle the nuts on the cheese mounds, if desired. Serves 4 to 6.

My contribution was often baked beans, not because I couldn't cook anything else, but I was told I made good beans—to take beans, so I took beans. Although I bake soybeans now, this was my baked bean recipe then, really my mother's.

HOME-BAKED BEANS

2 pounds any baking beans	2 teaspoons salt
7 tablespoons molasses	¾ pound salt pork or bacon
1 tablespoon dry mustard	1 large onion

Soak the beans overnight with water to cover. Parboil them until the skins crack, then pour them into a crock with liquid to barely cover, and stir in the molasses and seasoning. Cut up the salt pork or bacon, quarter the onion, and bury the pieces in the top of the beans. Cover and bake in a medium oven all day.

While we are on the subject of beans, how about a bowl of chili in this nippy weather?

CHILI CON CARNE

1 onion, chopped	4 cups cooked kidney beans or
1 green pepper, chopped	soybeans
1 celery stalk, chopped	2 teaspoons or more chili powder
1 clove garlic, chopped	1 teaspoon or more salt
2 tablespoons corn oil	2 cups canned tomatoes
1 pound ground chuck	2 teaspoons Worcestershire or
	soy sauce

Sauté the onion, pepper, celery, and garlic in oil 2 or 3 minutes. Add the meat, and sauté and stir about 5 minutes. Add the other ingredients and a little water or bean liquid if a soupier consistency is desired; cover and simmer 10 to 20 minutes more. Serve with coleslaw or green salad and crusty garlic bread. Makes 4 generous servings.

Well, it happened—a heavy frost. The best the weatherman gave us the night before was "scattered frost," and I was so involved in several projects that it was almost dark before I gave the matter serious thought. The clincher was a painful leg from sciatica. I decided to take a chance and stay put. I lost—but not without a fight.

Up at seven the next morning, I dressed hurriedly and headed for the porch to view the garden. It was covered with a thick white frost. Hobbling outside, I got the hose George had coiled up and put away, connected all the lengths, and turned on the water. I had heard that frozen vegetables could sometimes be redeemed if sprinkled with water before the hot sun hit the garden. The sun was almost at the tomatoes.

Usually we have very little pressure in the outside faucet, as it is hooked to a well with an inadequate pump. For all my trouble, a trickle of water came out of the hose, but I managed to wet three green tomatoes. Then I checked back and found the couplings leaking.

By this time, my feet were soaking wet and I was cold and miserable. George picked that moment to come out. I vented my spleen, chucked the whole thing, and stalked into the house as forcefully as I could with a gimpy leg. The heck with the golden midget watermelons, too! What we had picked would have to do.

Since the refrigerators were full of cucumbers, I decided to freeze some for the winter. The end product is no comparison to the fresh, but better than nothing and does give the cucumber flavor to winter salads. Anyway, it's an improvement over the questionable waxed and tasteless specimens found in markets in the winter at exorbitant prices.

FROZEN CUCUMBER CUBES

Put unpeeled cucumbers through the coarse blade of a food chopper and freeze them immediately in ice cube trays with the cube dividers in place. When frozen, remove from the trays, place the cubes in plastic bags, and return to the freezer. To use these when fresh cucumbers are not available, partially thaw the desired number of cubes, then crush and add to coleslaw and salads. Last year I ran out of ice cube trays, so froze some in 3-ounce paper cups.

It is now the season for nuts, so naturally I hit the road again. I did not fare very well. Nut trees seem to be temperamental in this area —one never knows when to expect a good year. Fortunately, I have a considerable supply of butternuts left from the five bushels we gathered several years ago, after Babe found an abandoned grove at the back of an old pasture. I still shudder when I remember how we almost fell apart carrying bushel after bushel of them to the outpost where the truck was parked.

Butternuts are fine, but my unchallenged favorite is the hickory nut. Would that I could find a new supply! Ozzie has two trees on the hill, and when they bear, I have the privilege of picking the crop.

My young friend who recently had the outdoor wedding discovered two black walnut trees on her property and offered to share the harvest with me. I'm eagerly waiting to take advantage of her generosity.

I have cracked many a nut during winter nights in the past, storing some in containers in the freezer to keep them fresh. Last week I reached the end of my freezer cache, so unveiled my nutcracking concrete block, set up my stool on the porch, and hammered away. In the past, this task was performed in the kitchen, and it was very trying for George. He would sometimes lose his sense of humor as he crunched shells underfoot that had sprayed over the floor while I was cracking. It was also difficult for him, a conventional person, to explain to winter visitors why we used a concrete block and a cardboard carton as part of our kitchen decor. The carton, resting behind the block, was for shells that failed to get away. George was relieved, with the advent of the porch, to see me transfer my nut-cracking paraphernalia there.

My method of shelling nuts is to place each in a groove worn in the block, point up, and then whack it with a hammer. Hickory nuts are easy to shell, often coming out in perfect halves. But the butternut is a tougher nut to crack—messier, often spraying shells over the floor.

I'd sure like to go nutting with Euell Gibbons, the expert on wild things edible. He says to raid hickories that grow in pastures, along fencerows, or otherwise away from other trees, as those growing among other trees have scant crops. I should be so lucky as to have a choice! I wonder how he finds such bounty?

I read recently that he uses the same method as I do to crack wild nuts, though he never mentioned a block. Maybe he cracks them outside on rocks. He did give out a hint for easy shelling of hickory nuts, which I shall try when hickories are again available. He said to freeze the nuts for a day, then shell a few at a time while they are frozen, striking them with a hammer just hard enough to crack the shell without smashing them. He claimed the kernels would come out in halves most of the time.

Though I found no nuts on my trip, I did scare a pheasant and a chipmunk, besides getting much needed exercise in the brisk autumn air. I was hungry when I reached home, so created a snack using some of my hoarded butternuts.

NUTTY APPLE RINGS

1 cup flour	2 eggs
½ teaspoon salt	⅓ cup milk
1½ teaspoons baking powder	2 tablespoons honey or sugar
2 tablespoons powdered milk (optional)	¼ cup finely chopped nuts
	2 tart apples

Combine the dry ingredients. Beat the eggs, milk, and honey or sugar, then stir into the dry ingredients and nuts to make a batter.

Peel, core, and slice the apples in ¼-inch rings. Dip the rings in the batter and fry them in oil. (Thin the batter with more milk if necessary.) Serve the rings with maple syrup or honey. I used whole wheat flour.

Here is another dandy nut pastry.

NUTTY PINWHEELS

2 eggs
½ cup milk
⅓ cup corn oil
2 tablespoons honey or sugar

3 cups flour (about)
¼ cup powdered milk (optional)
1 tablespoon baking powder
½ teaspoon salt

Filling:

¼ cup brown sugar
½ cup chopped nuts
raisins

Beat together the eggs, milk, oil, and honey. Add the combined dry ingredients, and knead into a medium dough. Cover and set aside while you mix together the brown sugar and nuts for the filling.

Roll out ½ the dough into a rectangle as thin as pie dough. Brush it with a mixture of melted butter and oil, and cut into long strips about 2 inches wide. Spoon the filling mixture along the center of the strip. then dot with raisins about 3 inches apart. Seal the sides by pinching the edges together to make a long tube. Starting at one end, roll each tube into a pinwheel, tucking the other end under.

Arrange the pinwheel spirals about 1 inch apart on a baking sheet, and bake at 350° about 30 minutes. When cool, frost with thin sugar icing and sprinkle with more ground nuts. To make icing, add plain or evaporated milk to about 1 cup of confectioners' sugar a little at a time until a thin icing results.

This pastry sounds like a lot of work but really isn't. It's fun to make and very yummy.

I had all sorts of adventures one Sunday when all I wanted was to enjoy the warm fall day by trimming the pine trees in our woods near Gail's camp off the road. In the fall, one isn't hassled by bugs—or so I thought. Although I had all sorts of things to do, I let everything go, got a hand axe, and went into the woods. The last time I trimmed dead branches off trees, Gail was with me, this time I went alone.

Before leaving, I had grabbed up a plastic pail for any goodies that crossed my path, and I collected three varieties of mushrooms, one I was pretty sure was edible. (I'm still trying to identify edible wild mushrooms by using a mushroom guidebook the Thornes gave me last Christmas. I haven't had the courage to eat any yet, especially since George is against my taking such chances until I am absolutely sure.)

After hacking away at the branches, I piled them up in one area and was generally enjoying myself when a nasty insect—I think a wasp or yellow jacket—bit my head and got tangled in my hair. Or I thought it did. Frantically combing my fingers through my hair, I ran all the way home and screamed to George to run out with a comb.

As soon as I recovered and stopped fingering my lump, I walked to the Andersons' house on an errand, and on the way back found a dead partridge in the road. I picked up the bird, still warm, and considered dressing it off, but decided against it when I found her injuries were too severe.

November

THE TREES in the swale are glowing in fall hues from bright yellow to deep scarlet. I hope it is the beginning of a warming trend that may last through the winter, but I heard that the *Farmer's Almanac* is predicting a winter of heavy snows. Heaven forbid! I am cringing already at the thought of hazardous winter driving from our outpost "21-acre farm and buildings" in the hills.

At last I have finished making all the pickles, relishes, and preserves. We are still pulling carrots and beets, cutting broccoli, and picking hardy herbs such as parsley, chives, and sage. I potted others. During the winter I shall have fresh, dried, and frozen herbs.

I have taken up jogging on our country road to tone up muscles that have turned to flab and to improve my circulation, which is threatening to stop from too much sitting. The lovely weather is an inducement, and since our area is not thickly populated I need not worry over making a spectacle of myself.

We are spreading manure laced with lime over the rear of the garden where plants have been pulled out since the freeze. I'm leaving most of this smelly job to George.

The pine grove beyond the porch needed trimming, so I took advantage of an Indian summer day to putter around there. Since taking an office job I have usually devoted the little time I have at home to the other most pressing needs when I'm not gardening.

Today I suddenly realized that I had not really paid attention to the grove for a long time.

When we first arrived here, we found the pine seedlings hidden in a patch of brambles, and cleared the area to give the trees a chance to grow. Later, we enlarged the lawn to include the pines, which border the swale at one end. Each year as they grew, we trimmed the lower branches. Unfortunately, the only time we can enjoy the grove is in the fall after the insect harassment dies down.

After an hour of chopping, sawing, and clipping while George went in to town, I took a lawn chair to the grove and sat down to listen to the painted leaves falling from the deciduous trees nearby. They made a sound like gentle summer rain. Suddenly a chipmunk scampered in front of me and disappeared into the lawn some distance away. Keeping my eyes on the spot, I walked to it and found a hole in the ground. Just then, the chipmunk's head emerged from the hole; he saw me and disappeared again. I returned to my chair and watched him run back and forth storing acorns for winter consumption. He shouldn't run short this year. I can't remember ever seeing so many acorns—they're still dropping from the oak trees. The roadsides are covered with them.

That reminds me ... Ozzie's hickory trees began shedding their nuts early and I completely missed the first batch, lost forever to either squirrels or chipmunks or someone passing by who noticed the nuts on the road and under the trees. Since then I have been stopping there regularly on my way home from the office, and I've accumulated enough to warrant setting up my cracking block again.

At the edges of one of our fields I planted a few black walnuts and hickory nuts. The old farmers claim most of the so-called wild trees by stone walls grew from nuts buried by chipmunks and squirrels, which took root. Since I am enjoying the harvest from some of those trees, I think it fair to plant nuts for the next generation. Gail came home with two friends in time to do more nut planting.

Last weekend I made a chicken salad spread so that our guests would have a filling for a quick sandwich or snack between meals. I never use or serve cold cuts or other such meat for sandwiches, as the sodium nitrite and sodium nitrate added to it turn me off. Here are the spread and a really delicious chicken soup made with the broth from cooking the fowl.

CHICKEN SALAD

1 cooked fowl or chicken	½ cup sunflower seed meal
1 cup (or more) chopped celery	juice of ½ lemon
1 small chopped onion	mayonnaise
¼ to ½ cup chopped fresh parsley	salt and pepper

Discard the fat and put the chicken meat—and skin, if desired—through the food chopper. Combine with the other ingredients and blend thoroughly. I use my homemade garlic mayonnaise. Use finely chopped nuts if sunflower seed meal is not available.

CHICKEN SOUP WITH LEMON-EGG SAUCE

1½ quarts chicken broth	1 egg
¼ cup brown or white rice	juice of ½ lemon
1 stalk celery and leaves, chopped	salt and pepper
¼ cup vermicelli (about)	cooked chicken (optional)

Skim the fat off the broth, bring broth to a boil, and add the rice and celery. When the rice is almost cooked, add the vermicelli and simmer until that is cooked. In a small bowl, beat the egg and lemon juice.

When the soup is done, remove it from the fire and add a small amount of the hot soup to the lemon sauce, stirring the sauce to prevent the egg from cooking; then stir the sauce into the soup. The trick is to keep the egg from flaking in the soup. This soup should be thick. If the soup is too thin I add more vermicelli, which cooks in a few minutes, before combining the soup with the sauce. If chicken meat is used also, cut it in small pieces and add it to the soup in time to heat through before combining with the sauce. Makes 4 to 6 servings.

Chicken is not only one of the best buys in this time of inflation but, I hope, the meat least polluted with DES (diethylstilbestrol). The practice of injecting poultry with DES pellets was banned by the Food and Drug Administration in 1959. However, other questionable practices are still permitted. Perhaps the only way to insure pure food is to grow and raise your own.

Here are more fowl or chicken recipes.

CHICKEN CHOP SUEY

2 cups slivered onions	1 cup snow peas (optional)
2 cups sliced celery	1 cup chicken broth
4 tablespoons corn or soy oil	1 to 2 cups cooked chicken
1 can or 2 cups bean sprouts	2 tablespoons or more soy sauce

Chop the onions and celery at an angle, similar to the way vegetables are prepared by Chinese restaurants. I do all my chopping with a Chinese chopper, which looks like a meat cleaver with a thinner blade.

Sauté the onions and celery in oil about 10 minutes. Add fresh bean sprouts (if used), snow peas, broth, and chicken, then soy sauce. If fresh sprouts are not available, add canned sprouts after the other vegetables are crunch-cooked, since the canned sprouts are already cooked. Also, substitute the liquid from the canned sprouts for the broth if you have no broth. Do not overcook the vegetables. Thicken the chop suey with about 1 rounded tablespoon cornstarch dissolved in a little water, cold broth, or sprout liquid. Serve with rice or chow mein noodles. Makes 4 generous servings.

Want to make your own fried noodles? Cook large egg noodles according to the package directions. Blot them dry and fry a few at a time in hot oil until crisp.

CHICKEN WITH CORN AND NOODLES

Meat from 1 fowl or chicken	1 cup noodles
6 cups chicken broth	½ cup or more cream
lump of butter	salt and pepper
2 or 3 cups fresh corn	

Cook the fowl or chicken in 2 quarts of water, or use canned chicken broth and boned chicken. Or cook chicken necks and backs for the broth and steam a broiler for meat.

Heat the broth, add the chicken and butter (or leave in an equivalent amount of chicken fat), then corn cut from the cob or frozen kernel corn. When the pot begins to boil, add the noodles, preferably homemade. Cover and cook 12 to 15 minutes. Before serving, stir in the cream and season. This is a very old southern recipe and a bit high caloried. Modify it as desired. Makes 4 to 6 servings.

The following recipe starts with the same ingredients, chicken and broth, and again utilizes a fowl. Perhaps I lean to fowl recipes because one year, when money was our scarcest commodity, we ended up with fifty tough old birds that had stopped laying, and we decided to eat them. I should have written down all the different ways I devised to cook fowl, to use for a separate cookbook. When we had finished off the fifty, I didn't serve fowl again for years.

CHICKEN STEW WITH DUMPLINGS

1 fowl or chicken
2 quarts water
2 cups canned or fresh tomatoes
2 sliced onions
2 cups corn kernels

1 cup cooked lima beans or
  raw green beans
1 clove garlic
salt and pepper

Cook an old hen in water (or get together the meat and broth another way). Skim off most of the fat, and return the cut-up boned chicken meat to the broth. Add the canned or skinned, cut fresh tomatoes, onions, corn, cooked lima beans or raw green ones, minced garlic, and seasoning. Simmer about 15 minutes and serve with or without dumplings, as desired. Makes 4 to 6 servings.

DUMPLINGS

2 cups flour
1 tablespoon baking powder
2 tablespoons powdered milk
  (optional)

1 teaspoon salt
1 cup milk
¼ cup corn oil

Combine the dry ingredients and fold in the milk and oil. Drop the dumplings on the top of the stew from a tablespoon moistened in the hot stew. Cover at once and simmer 12 to 15 minutes over low heat without removing the cover. Use a Dutch oven or large heavy pot with cover when making dumplings.

CHICKEN WITH BROWN RICE

1 broiler or parts
3 tablespoons corn oil
1 large onion, chopped
1¼ cups brown rice
3 cups hot water or chicken
   broth

1 stalk celery and leaves, chopped
1 green pepper, chopped
   (optional)
½ cup nut pieces (optional)

In a chicken fryer or other large heavy pot with a tight cover, sauté the onions in oil for 2 or 3 minutes. Add the rice and stir to coat each grain. Add the other ingredients, season with salt and pepper, and set the chicken pieces on top. Cover, bring to a boil, and let simmer until most or all the liquid is absorbed and the rice is cooked, about 1 hour. If necessary, add a little more liquid. For a spicier dish, add a little curry powder with the seasoning. Serve with a green salad. Makes 4 generous servings.

Years ago, we raised our own broilers, too, and I can still remember the difference in the flavor of the meat, which we attributed to the fact that our birds ran on open range and got no chemicals in their feed. The biggest hassle was dressing them off. I became an expert at picking feathers and gutting chickens. Even Gail got into the act, although she was hardly ten years old at that time.

We had various animals then, and the boys would rise early, don work clothes, and feed the hens, slop the pigs, and give hay to the sheep. Then they would wash and change into school clothes—all before I got out of bed. Their enthusiastic diligence petered out when they were in high school and discovered girls.

Babe was more dedicated to the farming scene than Dave. He spent a lot of time on a large working farm nearby, gleaning useful lore from one of the seven children there, a lad named Teddy.

One day while he was there, the two of them found a chicken with a packed crop—a condition that causes a hen's crop to harden and bloat, I think from eating too much long grass or something. The boys, then about thirteen and fourteen years old, decided to operate on the hen and clean out the crop. Babe told me, years later, that Teddy got a needle and thread from the house and a sharp knife, and they operated on the hen and sewed up her empty crop.

The hen lived through the operation but suddenly began to wilt, so Teddy ran into the house and returned with an eye-dropper and a little applejack. One of the boys held the hen's beak open while the other put a few drops of applejack down her throat. Babe said the hen let out one big squawk and keeled over dead. Both boys were shattered. They decided to give the hen a decent burial, for two reasons—to compensate for their surgical malpractice and to cover up the hen's demise.

Before we leave the chickens, here are two recipes of Gail's, which guests invariably request.

SWEET-SOUR ORIENTAL CHICKEN

1 broiler chicken, cut up
2 tablespoons corn oil
1¼ teaspoons salt
2 tablespoons water
1 sliced onion
1 tablespoon cornstarch
¼ cup vinegar
12-ounce jar of apricot, plum, or peach jam
1 tablespoon soy sauce

½ teaspoon ground ginger
1 green pepper, diced
1 tomato, cut in wedges
1 5-ounce can water chestnuts, sliced, or substitute about ½ cup sliced Jerusalem artichokes
½ cup sliced mushrooms (optional)

In a large chicken fryer or heavy stainless steel pot, brown the chicken in oil. Sprinkle with 1 teaspoon of the salt, add water, cover, and simmer 45 minutes. Remove the chicken and keep it hot. Cook the onions in the same pot. Dissolve the cornstarch in a little cold water and blend with the vinegar, jam, soy sauce, ginger and remaining salt. Add this mixture to the onions and cook until thick. Return the chicken to the pot; add pepper, tomato, chestnuts or Jerusalem artichokes, and mushrooms, if used, and heat. Serve with rice or noodles. Makes 4 generous servings.

CHICKEN LIVERS WITH WINE

1 pound chicken livers
4 tablespoons mixed oil and butter
1 large onion, coarsely chopped
1 green pepper, diced
¼ teaspoon dry basil

¼ teaspoon curry powder
1 cup chicken broth
½ cup dry vermouth or other dry wine
1 tablespoon cornstarch
salt and pepper to taste

Remove fat and tissue from the livers and separate the lobes. Sauté the onion and pepper in the butter and oil mixture about 5 minutes; add the livers and fry until barely cooked. Add seasoning, broth, and wine and heat to the boiling point. Thicken with the cornstarch dissolved in a little water. Spoon over cooked noodles or rice. Makes two very generous servings.

We pulled up all the old plants in the garden and piled them on the compost heap. I spent part of Sunday spreading hay over half the garden. George will finish the job during the week. The root crops were pulled earlier and stored for eating, as long as they last.

I shall now concentrate on my indoor garden on the porch. I have two Pixie tomato plants growing in one compartment of the huge plant gizmo, hybrid pickling cucumbers coming up in another, fresh herbs in the third, and an eggplant in the fourth. I threw a few old eggplant seeds in the last section in the spring, when it was empty, just to see if they would germinate. Several plants did and I pulled all but one out.

As I look out the window, I can see our once-bountiful dwarf fruit trees now bare, except for a coating of white fluff clinging on their branches as the season's first wet snow silently falls. Such pristine beauty, but it's a harbinger of winter, and dark thoughts of hassling transportation clutter the mind.

Since Jan, my daughter-in-law, sent me a stainless steel steamer from Florida, I have been on a vegetable steaming binge. This method of cooking preserves vitamins and the vegetables are much tastier. Sautéing chopped, shredded, or cubed vegetables quickly in oil the Oriental way also preserves vitamins.

One of our first acquisitions the summer we came here and stayed was a pair of pigs, Cynthia and Christopher. We got them when they were a few weeks old but named them when, as shoats, they had grown uglier and uglier. We tried to compensate with exotic names.

Before we brought them to the farm, where the boys and I were alone that summer, we had to build a pigpen. There was a small pig house on the farm but no fenced area outside. One weekend when George came to visit, we got a load of slabs free from a lumber mill, and brought the boards home in our panel laundry truck. Later, during the week, the boys and I built a pen.

At that time the boys were seven and nine years old, and my knowledge of carpentry was gleaned from a book. But the pen stayed together, even though the pigs finally grew to two hundred pounds and leaned against the sides.

It wasn't long before all the grass in the pen was gone and the bare ground had hardened like concrete, with depressions in several places where the pigs had bedded down and wallowed in the mud after a rain. One day Cynthia got wedged in such a depression under one end of the pig house. Babe noticed her predicament after he heard her squealing while he was out in the field. He alerted Dave and me, and we all stood by wondering what to do. Christopher was milling around restlessly inside and we though it wise not to trespass. Assuming we could divert Christopher, how could we dig Cynthia out of the concretelike earth?

I sent Babe to call a neighboring farmer, who came right over with his son and a grub hoe. I should explain here that a grub hoe is similiar to a pickaxe except that, instead of points at both ends, one end has a flat cutting edge.

Our neighbor, undaunted by Christopher, jumped into the pen and hacked Cynthia out in no time flat. Then he rigged the area under the pig house in a way to prevent a recurrence of the incident. And there never was one because in December that year both animals ended up in our freezer, disguised as bacon, ham, lard, pork loins, and chops—after special treatment from a butcher and smokehouse.

We kept pigs for several years but stopped when we decided to use the tie-up for sheep. At about this time of the year, when winter made the use of the pigpen a hardship for us, we would transfer the pigs to the tie-up for final fattening before butchering, usually in late December. Babe reminded me of another incident, which occurred when George, Dave, and he were transferring Rowena and Lancelot from the pen to the tie-up.

Some farmer had told them the easiest way to get a large pig from one place to another a short distance off was to make the animal back up all the way by putting a bushel basket over its head. In theory, the pig would back up to get out of the basket. Babe volunteered to walk forward with the basket over the pig's head while Dave and George guided the animal en route to the tie-up, a distance of about 30 feet. Nobody thought to explain the operation to Lancelot, who apparently had his own idea about the trip.

Anyhow, the three of them got Lancelot out of the pen and started toward the barn. As Babe tells it, "I don't know what happened—the next thing I knew, I was riding Lancelot backward and ended up near the edge of the pasture!"

Speaking of the pigs has reminded me of two favorite recipes with leftover ham.

HAM AND CORN CHOWDER

1 large onion, chopped	1 quart hambone stock or water
1 green pepper, chopped	1 package frozen or 1 can corn
1 stalk celery, chopped	ham pieces
2 tablespoons corn oil	1 pint milk or light cream
2 medium potatoes, sliced thin	salt and pepper

Sauté the onions, pepper, and celery in oil for 2 or 3 minutes. Add the potato slices and stock or water. (Taste the stock to be sure it is not too salty. Cut it with water if necessary.) Cook 10 minutes; then add the ham and corn and season. At this point, if desired, the chowder may be thickened with about 1 tablespoon cornstarch dissolved in a little water. Add milk or cream and heat, but do not boil. Makes about 4 servings.

HAM SALAD OR SANDWICH FILLING

4 cups chopped cooked ham	2 tablespoons chopped fresh dill
1 or 2 green peppers, chopped	fronds or few dill seeds
1 large onion, chopped	mayonnaise
½ cup chopped fresh parsley (optional)	salt and pepper to taste

Chop ham, onion, and green pepper by putting them through a food chopper. Add other ingredients and bind together with mayonnaise. Serve on lettuce with sliced tomatoes and cucumbers as a salad or make sandwiches with sour rye bread. Gail and a friend used some to make an omelet one morning.

We shall stay home this year at Thanksgiving, and I plan to invite all the family and relatives here. I hope they come, as our larder is full of all kinds of vegetables and nuts and the freezers with turkeys, fruits, and berries.

For the fourth year since I had the courage to try the slow-roast method of cooking the turkey, I shall gaily prepare the festive meal with no qualms about whether or not the bird is properly cooked. Actually, this will be the third year I have not been uptight over cooking the turkey. The first time I tried it, with guests yet, I was a nervous wreck until we cut the bird. It was worth it, though, because I found a better way to roast all meats.

For the benefit of anyone who would like to serve a tastier bird, here is the way I roast turkey. This method was recommended, after extensive research, by the National Live Stock and Meat Board and the U.S. Department of Agriculture.

SLOW ROAST TURKEY

Stuff the bird with your favorite dressing the night before. Brush all surfaces with oil. Do not salt. Place the turkey on a rack in a roasting pan. Roast for one hour in a preheated 300° oven, then lower the oven to 180° and go to bed.

If you have a reliable meat thermometer, you should remove the turkey from the oven when the thermometer registers 180° to 185°. If not, figure on roasting it about 3 times longer than the usual way. I usually put a 20-pound bird in the oven at 9 P.M. and take it out at 2 P.M. the next day. It won't hurt to cook it longer the slow way, as the meat won't dry out.

I almost forgot to mention: When you multiply the usual roasting time by three, to the total add the one hour during which the bird roasted at 300°. As I said before, exact timing isn't necessary, so cook it a little longer.

Don't expect any drippings for gravy after the turkey is done. Cook the neck and giblets separately in advance, drain the broth through a sieve, season, add a little Kitchen Bouquet or Gravy Master, and thicken with a mixture of flour and water shaken in a covered jar. Simmer the gravy covered to prevent a skin from forming.

To avoid doing everything in one day, I make all pies in advance and freeze them without baking. The day before Thanksgiving I thaw them, and then I bake them when the turkey comes out of the oven. No one has room for pie after dinner, so I leave them around for eating later or at suppertime.

FRUIT COCKTAIL

I also make my own version of fruit cocktail the day before by removing the peel and membranes from a couple of grapefruit and oranges and combining them with other fruit and berries. Into the huge glass bowl go cut-up peaches, pears, and several kinds of plums, apples, raspberries (all from our trees and bushes), sliced bananas, and crushed pineapple in its own juice. If I have grapes, I peel some and throw them in. Depending on whether the fruit is frozen or bottled, I add fruit juice or sweet cider if the mixture is too dry. If it needs sweetening, I add maple syrup or honey. To give the cocktail a subtle gourmet flavor, I shake in a few drops of Angostura Bitters. You should see the guests eat it!

Happy Thanksgiving! Go ahead and try the slow roast method. You won't regret it.

After I first experimented with the turkey, I tried roasting a face rump piece of beef the slow roast way, and we all enjoyed a new sensation in flavor. Again, I oiled all surfaces of the meat, a 4-pound piece, put it on a rack in a pan, roasted it for 1 hour in a preheated 300° oven to kill all bacteria, lowered the oven temperature to 180°, and left it in for 6 hours. It was done to perfection the way we like it—rare. I think it should bake 2 or 3 hours more for medium.

There is a theory behind the success of this method, but who cares? Take my word for it and risk the meat. You won't be sorry. I put the roast in at 10:30 A.M. and it was ready for our dinner at 5:30 P.M.

While I'm at it, a word about cooking fish. Fish has very little fat and when overcooked (as often happens), it becomes dry. Fish cooks faster than meat and care should be taken to remove it from the fire as soon as it is done. Although it should not be salted during cooking, other condiments such as pepper and paprika should be added for color. The juices can be retained if fillets are fried in oil in a batter.

BATTER-FRIED FISH FILLETS

1 pound fish fillets	½ teaspoon salt
½ cup whole wheat or white flour	1 egg, beaten
¼ cup powdered milk (optional)	¼ cup or more milk

Combine all ingredients except the fish with enough milk to make a batter of dipping consistency. Dip the fillets one by one, then fry them in oil.

Because we watch calories, we usually grill cod fillets.

GRILLED FLOURED FISH FILLETS

In a paper or plastic bag, combine ¼ cup whole wheat flour, 1 tablespoon powdered milk, and ¼ teaspoon dried basil or tarragon. Shake the fillets in the bag and let them dry for about 5 minutes to keep the crust from separating. Heat the grill and brush it with oil. Lay the fish on the grill and cook until golden underneath. Turn with a spatula and cook the other side. The whole process should take 8 to 10 minutes. Sprinkle the fillets with salt and lemon juice and serve with relish or tartar sauce.

Here is one of our favorite chowders. You have to taste it to believe it—it's so good!

FISH AND CORN CHOWDER

1 pound frozen cod fillets	½ teaspoon dried basil
1 large onion, chopped	1 teaspoon salt
4 tablespoons butter, or butter and corn oil	¼ teaspoon black pepper
	1 package frozen corn
1 large unpeeled potato, sliced	2 cups milk
1 cup water	

Sauté the chopped onion in butter for 2 minutes. Add the potatoes, water, basil, and seasoning. Simmer, covered, about 15 minutes. Cut the fish fillets into large cubes when they are partially thawed, and lay them over the potatoes. Cover and simmer until the fish flakes easily, about 10 minutes. Stir in the corn and cook 3 minutes more, then add milk and heat again. Serve with chopped parsley, sprinkled on top, if desired. Makes 4 servings.

One can of corn and its liquid, along with one tall can of undiluted evaporated milk, may be substituted for the frozen corn and fresh milk.

I was almost outwitted by a field mouse that moved into our house recently. He made his presence known in subtle ways, such as eating the oil-soluble vitamins I left in an open container on the kitchen table, which turned him into Mighty Mouse.

When I first remarked that some vitamins from our daily assortment were missing, George implied that I had reached the age of senility and I almost believed him. The next morning Gail, who had stayed overnight, said a mouse had sashayed into the living room from the kitchen while she watched late television. He disappeared under the sofa, she said.

George dug out our one rusty mousetrap, set it with a piece of cheese, and put it on the floor under the kitchen table. Two days later, since nothing had happened, I decided Mighty Mouse didn't like cheese. Nuts might have done the trick but, for the first time in years, I was fresh out of nuts. Then I remembered I had some sunflower kernels in a small apothecary jar on the counter.

Would you believe the jar was open and Mighty Mouse had eaten a quarter of the contents? I didn't—so I put the glass top back on the jar. Three hours later, in broad daylight, I glanced at the jar and saw that the cover was tipped to one side, but not opened this time. Mighty Mouse either gave up or probably heard me coming.

I closed the jar again, and that night George moved the cheese-set trap onto a paper towel in front of the jar. The next morning, I glanced in the general direction of the trap. Without my glasses, my vision is rather a blur, so I slowly crept closer. Mighty Mouse had eaten the cheese without tripping the trap and finished his meal with sunflower seeds for dessert!

George oiled and reset the trap. I thought of bringing in one of the cats but, in view of their past performances, decided to stick with the trap a little longer. Since we had got no positive results with the trap, however, George decided it was defective and bought a new one and set it.

I was finishing a bath that night (our bathroom is off the kitchen; it was formerly the cold pantry) when, through the closed door, I heard a rattle from the kitchen. At first I thought it was George, but remembered I had left him in the living room watching the news on television; the sound was coming from the general direction of the set trap. Calling to George, I told him to check the trap. He did—found

Mighty Mouse in it and, acting like a sports announcer, gave me a blow by blow description of the rodent's last challenge. Fortunately, any chance Mighty Mouse had to sire a super-race died with him.

December

I CLIMBED the ladder into the loft over the utility room, once our woodshed, to get the Christmas wrappings this past weekend, and stayed two hours, rediscovering all sorts of treasures stored there years ago and since forgotten.

The back end of the house is much tighter now than it was when we first came as summer people. When that end was the woodshed, it had a dirt floor and large cracks in the boarded back wall. I remember how I studied the cracks at that time and decided they were too wide to have resulted from shrinkage. Finally I asked a neighbor about them. He said the wall had purposely been left open to allow air to dry the stored wood, which might not always have been thoroughly seasoned. That made sense, so I didn't give the wall further thought—at least, not until the night of the thumping.

A friend and her two sons, slightly younger than Babe and Dave, who were six and eight then, came to visit one week. Newly arrived from the noisy city, she and I both feared the dead silence and the black nights, especially as we had no resident menfolk to protect us.

The privy was at the far end of the woodshed, directly opposite the back kitchen door. As country privies go, it was surely one of the more attractive ones, with double facilities painted in gray enamel and a gray and white wallpaper with sprays of lilac. In daylight, from the square window, you had a lovely view of mountains, fields, and trees.

On this particular night of Flossie's visit, we had washed the children and were ready to put them to bed, mine upstairs with me and Flossie's in the first-floor bedroom with her. I was about to take a trip down the long boardwalk from the back door to the privy when we heard loud thumping sounds from the loft area over it, which extended over the kitchen too. Magnified by the thick silence, the sounds seemed to be those of some large, vicious animal that must have found a loose board, climbed in and then up to the loft.

Flossie and I stood in the kitchen as long as possible, quivering with fright. Eventually, seeing no alternative but to make a dash for it, each of us took a turn standing guard outside the kitchen door with the boys' baseball bat while the other made a fast run down the boardwalk to the privy and back—without mishap.

Since, in those days, the youngsters were always the first ones up in the morning, I warned them to stay away from that area until we had had a chance to investigate next morning. They disobeyed me, of course, their curiosity getting the best of them, climbed into the loft, and discovered a scared jackrabbit. In due time, we closed the cracks and clapboarded the back wall.

This house had been empty for two years when we moved in that summer. By a stroke of luck, at my mother's suggestion, we did bring the two abandoned cats with us on the first memorable moving trip.

We kept the cats in the house here for a week. Only Babe and Dave slept soundly. My mother and I slept fitfully, and I don't think the cats slept at all. Every morning we found a heap of mouse tails in the middle of the bare floor of the living room. We never found the rest of the mouse bodies—the cats had good appetites. The tail pile diminished daily, and finally we decided the cats could stay outside.

We still hear mice in the walls once in a while, but I think most of them now winter in the garden under the fresh hay we spread in the fall. They subsist on the parsley roots, Jerusalem artichokes, and sometimes young fruit-tree bark. Maybe we need mice for the balance of nature, but offhand I can't think what purpose they serve.

I made some of my mother's lemon snaps, using her old Christmas cookie cutters, to hang on the tree for young visitors and old, too. There were Santas, stars, bells, and Christmas trees. And while the oven was on, I baked a casserole of spiced quartered apples, drizzling honey over the quarters and sprinkling them with mixed spices. I have a simple method of getting apples peeled and quartered or sliced. I take the apples and a knife to George while he watches a football game.

LEMON SNAPS

½ cup butter	1 tablespoon milk
¾ to 1 cup sugar	1 teaspoon baking soda
1 egg	½ teaspoon salt
1 lemon, juice and grated rind	unbleached flour
grated rind of 1 orange (optional)	

Cream the butter and sugar; add the egg, lemon juice, and grated rinds. In a cup, stir the milk and soda together, then add them to the creamed mixture. Add the salt and sufficient flour to make a dough stiff enough to roll out. (Too much flour will make the cookies tough.) Before baking, pierce each cookie with a hole for hanging. Bake at 350° for 10 to 15 minutes, depending on thickness.

This cookie, which became a favorite with my family, was made by my mother when I was a little girl. Everyone who has eaten it asks for the recipe. I sometimes substitute honey for part of the sugar and use corn oil margarine instead of butter, or sneak in a little stone-ground whole wheat flour. George notices and grumbles, preferring the original recipe, but eats them anyway.

Here are more excellent cookie recipes for Christmas giving or eating.

ZINGY GINGERSNAPS

1½ cups butter or part	4 cups flour
corn oil margarine	2 teaspoons baking soda
2 cups sugar or part honey	2 teaspoons cinnamon
2 eggs	2 teaspoons cloves
½ cup molasses	2 teaspoons ginger

Cream the butter, add the sugar gradually, and beat until light. Thoroughly beat in the eggs and molasses. Combine the dry ingredients and gradually add them to the batter, which will be on the soft side. Make 1-inch balls with the hands, and place them 3 inches apart on a cookie sheet. (Roll the balls in sugar first, if desired.) Bake at 375° for 12 to 15 minutes. This recipe makes a large quantity, but it can be cut in half.

I bake all cookies on ovenliners made of heavy foil. They work fine if handled carefully, cool almost instantly, and are easy to clean.

After eating more gingersnaps than necessary to find out how they tasted, I discoved that my ginger had lost its zing. I'm not surprised, since this batch has been around a long time. I shall replace it with fresh-ground ginger.

MINCEMEAT-HONEY DROP COOKIES

½ cup butter or corn oil margarine	3 cups flour
⅓ cup corn oil	¼ cup wheat germ
1 cup sugar	½ teaspoon salt
½ cup honey	1 teaspoon baking soda
2 or 3 eggs	1¼ cups prepared mincemeat
	nut pieces (optional)

Cream together the butter, oil, sugar, and honey. Add the eggs. Combine the dry ingredients and add them. Then add the mincemeat and nuts, if used. Drop by teaspoonfuls on a cookie sheet, and bake at 375° about 12 minutes. I never grease cookie sheets but do loosen the cookies with a spatula immediately after removing them from the oven.

HONEY-OATMEAL CRISPIES

¾ cup butter or corn oil margarine	1 teaspoon baking powder
1 cup or less sugar	½ teaspoon baking soda
½ cup honey	1 teaspoon salt
2 large eggs	1 teaspoon mixed cinnamon and nutmeg or only cinnamon
2 cups quick oats	1 cup mixed raisins and nuts
2 cups flour	

Cream the butter and sugar. Add the honey and eggs. Combine the dry ingredients and add. Stir in the raisins and nuts. Drop by teaspoonfuls on a cookie sheet and press a nut in the center of each cookie, if desired. Bake at 350° for 12 to 15 minutes.

I use less than a cup of sugar, as we like cookies less sweet. Sometimes I substitute stone-ground whole wheat flour for ½ the flour or all of it. Other times, I substitute ¼ cup wheat germ for part of the flour, or some soya powder too. Try an innovation of your own.

We have no Christmas trees on our farm, but heard there were some on a nearby piece of land we bought recently, so Gail and I prepared to go cut one for the holiday. At the time, George was in California visiting relatives.

Ozzie, our stalwart neighbor at Hillside Orchards, offered to accompany us, and we welcomed his help gratefully. There was considerable walking before we could get into the woods, and I was suspicious about my ability to negotiate the trek, being out of condition, as usual. I don't know what I expected Ozzie to do about it, but at least his presence would give me moral support.

Ozzie brought a saw and pruning shears, and the three of us set off, with him leading the way. We plowed through the deep snow, over fallen logs, through a double barbed-wire gap, down an abandoned road, sometimes walking and sometimes sliding, trailing behind Ozzie, who had long legs. After what seemed to be a mile but was probably a city block, we came to the gap in the stone wall at the edge of the woods. Ozzie went on ahead and we followed his footprints in the snow. On and on we trudged, with nary a Christmas tree in sight.

Gail stopped to look around, applying her recent study of dendrology, but saw no sign of a spruce. Ozzie had long since disappeared—he was completely out of sight.

As I reached the point of collapse, I suggested stopping and just waiting for Ozzie to return. To heck with the tree—it was obvious we'd been given a bum steer.

Finally, Ozzie's "view halloo" joined my panting breath to break the thick silence of the woods. I shouted back. He retraced his footsteps to where we were leaning against trees.

"I found a clump of spruce up ahead a piece," he said.

"Did you cut one?" I asked.

"No. I thought you'd want to be along to pick one out."

"Forget it," I said. "Let's go home—we'll cut a pine or some other evergreen."

"You go on back. I'll look around a bit," said Ozzie.

We started back, guided by our footprints in the snow, grabbing onto branches to climb the hilly spots. Eventually we hit civilization and the road. As I stamped the snow off my boots, I saw Ozzie coming out of an old road with a sickly spruce in his hand and a wide grin on his face.

When we got home, Ozzie pruned the tree and stood it by our barn door. It was not as bad as I thought—it looked fine once we got it on the porch and trimmed it.

Taking advantage of Gail's holiday mood, I gave her a holiday bread recipe to bake, updating it with more nutritious ingredients. She had excellent results, turning out a tender prize loaf and swirls of her own invention, packed into a second loaf pan. Here is the recipe.

HOLIDAY BREAD OR BUNS

5 to 6 cups flour	¼ cup corn oil
1½ teaspoons salt	⅓ cup sugar or honey
2 packages dry yeast	2 large or 3 small eggs
¾ cup milk	1 cup mixed dried or
½ cup water	candied fruit and nuts

In a large mixer bowl, combine 2 cups of the flour, the salt, and yeast. Heat the milk, water, oil, and sugar or honey until very warm, and gradually add to the dry ingredients. Beat 2 minutes at medium speed. Add the eggs and more flour, to make a thick batter. Beat 2 minutes more. Then stir in more flour for a soft dough.

Oil your hands and knead the dough until it is smooth and elastic, about 10 minutes. Cover, and let rise until double in bulk. Knead in the fruit and nuts. Divide the dough in half and shape it into two loaves. Place them in oiled loaf pans and let rise again. Bake in a 350° oven about 45 minutes. Remove the loaves from the pans and cool on trivets. Frost with confectioners' sugar icing and decorate. To make the icing, gradually add enough plain or evaporated milk to 1 cup confectioners' sugar for a thin icing.

At my suggestion, Gail substituted 2½ cups fine-ground whole wheat flour for the same amount of unbleached flour and added 2 heaping tablespoons powdered milk to the dry ingredients. She used honey instead of sugar.

George made some fine-ground whole wheat flour for me by running my regular stone-ground whole wheat flour through our hand-crank coffee grinder, setting it on fine grind. Remember the one I got for twenty-five cents at the rummage sale?

Any type of sweet bread or rolls can be made with this sweet dough, combining jams, fruits, and berries with nuts. Try a braided loaf. For the fruit in the bread, Gail combined cut-up figs and dates with currants and hickory nuts. This bread, without icing, is great toasted.

Years ago, my mother made a date-nut bread for Christmas giving and eating. It's yummy, and easy to make.

DATE-NUT BREAD

1½ cups chopped nuts	1½ cups boiling water
2 cups cut-up dates	4 eggs
1 tablespoon baking soda	2 cups sugar
1 teaspoon salt	3 cups sifted unbleached flour
6 tablespoons corn oil	2 teaspoons vanilla

Combine the nuts, dates, soda, and salt, stirring together with a fork. Add the oil and water, and let stand for 20 minutes. Beat the eggs with a fork. Add the sugar, flour, and vanilla to the eggs, then add the date mixture. Pour into 2 oiled loaf pans and bake at 350° for 1 hour.

I haven't made this bread since I turned into something of a health nut, so have not updated it with more nutritious ingredients. Do try some innovations. This bread, cut in thin slices and spread with cream cheese, is super.

Our sickly Christmas tree, festooned with colored lights, baubles, cranberry-popcorn ropes, and shiny icicles, was a beautiful sight standing in the corner of the porch. Its reflection in the glass doors at night gave it added majesty, and its uneven branches, more character.

At the other end of the porch, there are two flowers on the cucumber vine in one section of the large planter. The tomato plants are in flower too, and I shake them periodically to pollinate the flowers, but use the paintbrush on the cucumber flowers.

When I dug into the planter to test the moisture in the soil, a worm reared its head. Fearing he and his friends would find little to eat, I buried bits of bread throughout the area. Well-fed, contented worms will breed better and enrich the soil, I theorized. Worms are hermaphrodites, with both male and female reproductive organs, and they lay eggs that resemble tiny lemons. Each egg hatches from five to ten worms. Worms break up hardpan and aerate the soil by eating and digesting it. Aristotle called them the intestines of the soil.

Preparing for a holiday open house, I made an easy honey-fig-nut cake; it was so tasty, I tried another version with dates.

The original recipe, which came from the Midwest a hundred years ago, was probably made with fresh-ground whole wheat flour. I made the fig cake with a mixture of unbleached flour and raw wheat germ, but used all stone-ground fresh whole wheat flour for the date version, adding ¼ cup powdered milk for extra nutrition. Both versions were excellent.

This cake can no doubt be made successfully with refined bleached flour too, but more and more I am leaning to the use of wholesome ingredients with all the vitamins intact. I hope I can influence other homemakers in the same direction. We are all inclined to go overboard on festive occasions—it seems to me better to do it nutritionally as well, when flavor is not sacrificed.

If figs are used to make this cake, soak one pound of them in boiling water to soften and, hopefully, wash off the fumigants. I used dry-strung figs and happened to notice that the label stated they were fumigated. After soaking, cut each fig in half and put aside.

FIG OR DATE-NUT CAKE

Use 1 cup, your choice, of one
of these flour mixtures:

1 cup whole wheat flour and 1 tablespoon soya powder *or*	1 cup flour, preferably unbleached, *or*
¾ cup flour and ¼ cup wheat germ *or*	any other combination to make 1 cup

2 teaspoons baking powder	3 large eggs, separated
⅛ teaspoon salt	1 pound pitted whole dates or soaked figs
¼ cup powdered milk (optional)	½ pound nuts, whole or in large pieces
1 cup sugar (or ½ cup each sugar and honey)	
1 teaspoon vanilla	

Combine the dry ingredients. Add the egg yolks and sugar (or sugar and honey); then vanilla, fruit, and nuts. Fold stiffly beaten egg whites thoroughly into the stiff batter. Pour into an oiled loaf pan lined with wax paper on the bottom, and bake at 300° about 1½ hours.

This cake, thinly sliced, shows the fruit and nuts in cross section, giving it an unusual appearance.

Years ago, on the old southern plantations, a confection known as "peach leather" was made from peach pulp or juice. I have never been able to track it down, but do make grape and apple leather that must be similar. A stack of this edible leather, with lengths or slices from a variation made with nuts, called *rojig*, should make an unusual Christmas gift item or a conversation piece when friends visit. Besides, it's fun and easy to make. For those who want to try it, these preliminary steps are necessary.

To make the leather, find a flat surface, preferably a large table, where the leather can dry for a couple of days without interference from insects. Spread the surface with several layers of newspaper topped with one or two pieces of clean old sheeting about a yard square, depending on whether you make only leather or the nut variation. Find some kind of implement to spread the mixture ⅛ to ¼ inch thick over the cloth—a wide spatula perhaps. It occurs to me that a small cement smoother would be ideal, but probably not sanitary. Never mind—stick to the spatula.

George had offered to make grape juice one day from our wild grapes on the stone wall, but when I arrived home I found he had made grape pulp instead. So I decided to make grape leather, for which either pulp or juice can be used. To make the pulp, which is faster, wash the grapes and pick them off the stems into a large, preferably enamel or stainless steel, pot. Add enough water to keep them from sticking to the pot, and cook until soft. Put through a Foley food mill, discarding the skins and seeds for the compost pile.

GRAPE LEATHER BASE

Malez

4 quarts grape pulp or juice	1 cup cornstarch
4 to 6 cups sugar (or part honey)	1 tablespoon salt
	1 teaspoon cinnamon
2 cups flour	½ cup cold water

Combine the sugar, flour, cornstarch, salt, and cinnamon in a large bowl, blending them thoroughly. To ½ cup of grape pulp, add the cold water, and gradually stir this liquid into the dry ingredients in the bowl. (If grape juice is used, substitute the juice for the water, as the only purpose of the water is to thin the pulp.) Add 3 more cups of grape pulp to the bowl mixture, stirring until smooth.

Put the remainder of the grape pulp in a large heavy pot and bring it to a boil, stirring occasionally. Gradually add the mixture from the bowl, and stir the brew until it reaches the boiling point. It has a tendency to stick to the bottom of the pot, so keep stirring over lower heat.

To make stirring with my large, long-handled spoon easier (my arm gets tired), I stand on a kitchen chair and grasp the spoon with two hands.

"I feel like one of the witches in *Macbeth*," I said to George, who was standing by ready to help.

He gave me the once-over. "You look it, too." I let that pass.

When the brew boils, remove it from the stove and let it cool for about 15 minutes, stirring occasionally.

George poured the thick brew on the sheeting and I spread it. Before it began to harden, I sprinkled hickory nut pieces over the leather. After two days, it was ready to hang for a few more days in a cold area (in our house, the utility room).

When it is dry, take the sheets back to the table and cut them into strips about 6 inches wide to facilitate separating the leather from the sheet. Turn one strip over at a time and sponge the cloth on the back generously with cold water; let set a couple of minutes, then turn the strip back over with the leather side up. Scrape a narrow end of the leather loose with a knife and peel the leather strip from the cloth. Lay each strip, wet side up, on the clean counter to dry while working on the next strip. After peeling off all strips, brush the damp side (the one that was against the cloth) with cornstarch. Then cut into squares, roll each strip up, or fold—whichever is convenient. If tougher leather to exercise the teeth is desired, leave it in the open to continue hardening. If not, store it in a metal container lined with wax paper, in a cold area, or refrigerate or freeze.

To make the nut variation, or rojig, shell 1 or 2 pounds of walnuts after letting them stand in boiling water for an hour so that the halves will remain as intact as possible. Or buy walnut halves in cans, using those that are large enough to string.

Thread halves and pieces, with a needle, on a piece of string about 18 inches long, knotted at one end. Keep the halves facing in the same direction, and leave at least 6 inches of string to tie onto a wooden suit hanger or dowel. Tie 3 strings of nuts on each hanger.

Dip the strung nuts into the cooled base mixture, holding them over the pot until most of the excess runs off. Then hang them over clean counter space to finish dripping. The drippings can be scraped up with a spatula and returned to the pot. Dip the nuts once or twice more, to thicken the coating. Allow them to dry a few days or longer in a cold area. After they are dry, cut the bottom knot, pull out the string, and cut in 4-inch lengths or slice when serving.

Apple leather base is made the same way, using the same proportions of ingredients. I haven't experimented with other juices but see no reason why they can't be used. I would add some lemon juice to such bland juices as pineapple. Sugar quantity is a matter taste and the tartness of the pulp or juice. I do a lot of tasting when cooking, to get the flavor just right. It's a good sneaky way to put on weight, too.

Nuts are optional on the leather but give it a gourmet touch. I have made it without nuts but eaten it with nuts. My method is to cut a square, line one edge with nuts, roll the square up tight, and start biting at one end.

Through various sources, I learned of the nutritional value of carob and decided to find some use for it, since I had an unused package of carob powder I had bought years earlier when I first went overboard on health foods. Carob is ground from the long dry pod of a honey locust tree, cultivated along the Mediterranean; it is also known as Saint-John's-bread.

The powder is alkaline, and has a high calcium content and low starch and fat—2 percent fat as compared to 52 percent in chocolate. Carob has more vitamin A than equal amounts of many vegetables. It contains natural sugars and minerals, such as calcium, phosphorus, iron, copper, and magnesium. Carob does not have the undesirable qualities of chocolate, which are too numerous to mention.

I noticed in a health food store that carob was substituted for chocolate in many of the candy bars. What the heck! I decided to try making candy and came up with these gems, very easy to make and no cooking. Jessica and Aram, my grandchildren in Florida, will get some in their Christmas package, as well as some grape and apple leather.

CAROB NUT ROLL

½ cup carob powder
½ cup soya powder
½ cup powdered milk
¾ cup sunflower seed meal
¾ cup sesame seed

2 tablespoons safflower or peanut
   oil
¾ cup honey
chopped nuts

Combine the carob, soya powder, powdered milk, sunflower seed meal, and sesame seed in a bowl. Add the oil and honey and knead with oiled hands. Shape the mixture into a long roll, coat with chopped nuts, and refrigerate. Slice to serve. I used sunflower seed meal because I had some on hand. Sunflower seeds can be substituted.

CAROB PEANUT-BUTTER CANDY

½ cup carob powder
½ cup sesame seed
½ cup sunflower seed meal
¼ cup soy grits or powder
¼ cup toasted wheat germ

¼ cup powdered milk
½ cup pure peanut butter
½ cup honey
unsweetened coconut *or*
   chopped nuts

Combine all but the last 3 ingredients. Add the peanut butter and honey, and knead together. Form in a roll and coat with coconut or nuts, or make small balls and roll them in the coconut or nuts.

If I had it to do all over again, and could cope with their grandmothers, I would satisfy my children's sweet tooth by giving them dried fruits such as raisins, dates, figs, and apricots instead of commercial candies. When Gail was in elementary school, I bought small boxes of raisins, emptied half of them out and substituted shelled nuts, making a tasty mixture. My mother often stuffed dates and figs with nuts, another nutritious confection for children.

Fresh fruit is another treat I would encourage, especially for children. Unless you grow your own, be sure to scrub off any harmful insecticide sprays before eating the fruit. Washing is a good idea regardless, since insects are likely to crawl over ripened fruit. Children who are never introduced to the commercial junk foods won't miss them and will find these simple treats satisfying.

If you have a source of raw peanuts, here is a dandy taste treat.

LIGHT-ROASTED PEANUTS

Spread the raw peanuts in one layer in a shallow tray, and roast them in a 300° oven for 15 minutes. That's all there is to it!

Here is another holiday treat for the children, easy to make and more nutritious than candy.

HOLIDAY POPCORN CRUNCH

½ cup honey
½ cup mixed butter and
  corn oil

3 quarts popped corn
1 cup nut pieces *or*
  peanuts

Heat the honey, butter, and oil until the butter melts, then pour over popcorn and nuts or peanuts. Mix well and spread on a cookie sheet in a thin layer. Bake in a 350° oven for 15 minutes. Remove from the oven and cool in the pan on a trivet; during the cooling the popcorn mixture will become crisp. Store in an airtight tin or plastic container. Better double the recipe—grown-ups will eat this too.

Since guests may drop in at any time in the holiday season, I keep a frozen supply of two favorite desserts, fast and easy to make. Whenever I'm baking, if I have used up my frozen supply of Fairy Food Cake or Easy Cupcakes, I mix up a batch to share the oven with whatever else I'm preparing.

FAIRY FOOD CAKE

4 eggs (separated)
7 tablespoons cold water
1½ cups sugar

1½ cups flour
1 teaspoon vanilla

Beat the egg yolks and water for about 3 minutes. Add the sugar and beat 3 minutes more. Add the flour and beat another 3 minutes. Fold in the stiffly beaten egg whites and vanilla. Pour in an ungreased tube pan and bake at 325° for 1 hour. After removing from the oven, invert the pan at once until the cake is cold.

This is a light cake that is delicious with a berry sauce or a light fluffy frosting. One-half cup honey may be substituted for part of the sugar, and a heaping tablespoon of soya powder for the same amount of flour.

The cupcake recipe may be varied in many ways. Sometimes I add carob to half of the batter, cutting the sugar a little and compensating by putting chopped nuts on the carob cupcakes before baking and icing the white cupcakes afterward. Other times I add raisins or another dried fruit.

EASY CUPCAKES

1¾ cups flour	⅔ cup milk
1 tablespoon baking powder	½ cup corn oil margarine
½ teaspoon salt	2 large eggs
1 cup or less sugar	1 teaspoon vanilla

Combine the flour, baking powder, salt, and sugar in a mixing bowl. Add the milk and margarine and beat about 2 minutes. Add the eggs and vanilla and beat 2 minutes more. Bake at 375° for 20 to 25 minutes.

I substitute soya powder and sometimes wheat germ for part of the flour. Or I may use part or all stone-ground whole wheat flour. I also add 3 tablespoons powdered milk to the dry ingredients and use honey for part of the sugar. Makes 15 large cupcakes. Since I put paper baking cups in a tin that holds just a dozen, I pour the extra batter in a small pie plate for a tiny cake.

Frost with basic confectioners' sugar icing (see index), flavoring part with cocoa if desired. Decorate with chocolate jimmies, colored sugar, coconut, nuts, or dried fruit.

Babe and Judy came to visit the day after Christmas, bearing gifts for us all. My gift was a triumph of ingenuity. Under the wrappings was a wicker wastebasket, orange to blend with the Mexican color scheme of the porch, filled with a myriad of gaily wrapped smaller packages.

During one of the rare occasions when I was speechless, I opened the packages one by one, to reveal delicacies some of which I never knew existed. Among them were Japanese shark fin soup, guava paste with jelly center, mung bean threads, watercress soup from France, seaweed from Japan, Hawaiian papaya slices, Norwegian ship biscuits, English heather honey, Ichiban Japanese-style alimentary paste with soup base, pure rose extract, Hawaiian macadamia nut brittle, fried green peas to "eat like salted nuts," and dried cherries.

We immediately sampled some of the goodies, relishing the new flavors. A sniff of the rose extract convinced the ladies that it would substitute for perfume, and we dabbed some behind our ears. I remain a little leery of the shark fins in soup. It may join the can of whale meat, still intact, that Gail sent us two years ago from California.

Judy brought a chocolate cake with her, and everyone raved over it. She could not remember the recipe, but promised to mail it. When it finally came, as I read it I thought of several changes to make it healthier. George, my born hash-house eater with no gourmet inclinations, protested. Bristling, I told him he did not have to eat the cake, and I huffed out to the utility room refrigerator to get my health ingredients. Frankly, I admit I am beginning to be incapable of following a regular recipe anymore without trying to make it healthier.

After I finished the cake, I cut a small piece and stuck it into George's mouth while he watched a football game on television. He voiced his approval in his usual enthusiastic manner: "Not bad," and headed for the kitchen to cut a large square.

Here are both versions of the cake.

JUDY'S CHOCOLATE CAKE

⅔ cup soft shortening	1 teaspoon vanilla
1⅔ cups sugar	2 cups flour
3 eggs	⅓ teaspoon baking powder
⅔ cup cocoa	1¼ teaspoons baking soda
1⅓ cups cold water	1 teaspoon salt

Cream the shortening and sugar together until fluffy, then beat in the eggs. Blend together the cocoa, water, and vanilla. Sift the remaining dry ingredients together. Beat them into the creamed mixture alternately with the cocoa-water mixture. Bake at 350° in a 13 x 9 inch pan, lined with wax paper, for 35 to 45 minutes. Frost with:

CHOCOLATE ICING.

To make the icing, add 2 cups confectioners' sugar alternately with about 3 tablespoons evaporated milk to ¼ cup corn oil or soft butter and beat until creamy. Flavor with 2 tablespoons or more plain cocoa.

HEALTHIER CHOCOLATE CAKE

⅔ cup corn oil margarine
1 cup sugar
3 eggs (separated)
1⅓ cups cold water
1 teaspoon vanilla
1 cup unbleached flour
1 cup stone-ground whole
  wheat flour

⅔ cup carob powder
¼ cup powdered milk
1 heaping tablespoon soya
  powder
¼ teaspoons baking powder
1¼ teaspoons baking soda
1 teaspoon salt

Cream the margarine and sugar together until fluffy. Beat in the egg yolks. Add the vanilla to the water. Sift or stir together the dry ingredients, then beat them into the creamed mixture alternately with the water-vanilla mixture. Fold in the stiffly beaten egg whites. Bake in the same manner as Judy's cake, in same size pan.

I reduced the amount of sugar because carob powder, which has a flavor like chocolate, is naturally sweet. If I hadn't got caught short without honey, I would have substituted honey for part of the sugar.

While we are on cakes, here is one of the best-ever butter cakes. We dubbed it "birthday cake" when I was still making it for the children. Every mother who tasted it asked for the recipe. This is the cake Gail made when we forced George to celebrate his birthday last August. I have listed the original recipe, along with my changes.

BIRTHDAY CAKE

1 cup butter
1½ cups sugar
3 eggs (separated)
3 cups sifted flour
½ teaspoon salt

¾ teaspoon baking soda
1¼ teaspoons cream of tartar
1 cup milk
1 teaspoon vanilla

Cream the butter and sugar well. Blend in the egg yolks. Combine the dry ingredients and add them to the creamed mixture alternately with the milk and vanilla. Fold in the stiffly beaten egg whites last. Bake in three layers or one large 10 x 13 inch pan, lined with wax paper. Bake the layers at 375° for 20 to 25 minutes, and the large pan at 350° about 50 minutes.

Instead of butter, I now use mostly corn oil margarine and substitute ½ cup honey for the same amount of sugar. Sometimes I use part stone-ground whole wheat flour, or substitute ¼ cup wheat germ and 2 tablespoons soya powder for the same amount of flour. I always add ⅓ cup powdered milk with the dry ingredients.

Frost with:

CONFECTIONERS' SUGAR ICING

5 tablespoons corn oil or soft butter	6 tablespoons evaporated milk (about)
few grains salt	1 teaspoon vanilla
1 pound confectioners' sugar	

Add confectioners' sugar alternately with evaporated milk to salt and oil or butter for a creamy consistency. Add vanilla. Spread thinly between layers and on top of cake. Decorate with chocolate jimmies, coconut, or chopped nuts.

I made a lemon pound cake recently from an 1850 recipe—with slight variations—on which George finally put his stamp of approval. Gail even added it to her recipe file.

I should explain that George considers himself a connoisseur of pound cake, his favorite in the cake family. Years ago, since none of my pound cakes were to his liking and I don't care for them anyway, I gave up attempting to please him and let him buy his pound cakes.

I found the 1850 recipe in a 1936 copy of *American Cookery Magazine,* published by the Boston Cooking School Company. It came in a box of old books and magazines for which I bid a quarter during an auction many years ago. When I emptied an old commode for Gail, I found it again. This is how I made the cake.

LEMON POUND CAKE

4 eggs (separated)
1 cup corn oil margarine
2 cups sugar
⅔ cup honey
1 large lemon

4 cups unbleached flour
1 teaspoon baking soda
4 tablespoons powdered milk (optional)
1 cup milk

I simplified the directions by separating the eggs first, beating the egg whites stiff, and setting them aside. Beat the egg yolks until thick and creamy, using the unwashed beaters after beating the egg whites. Put the beaten yolks aside. In a large mixing bowl, cream the margarine, then gradually add the sugar and honey, still using the same unwashed beaters. If honey is not available, use all sugar.

Next, add the egg yolks, juice and grated rind of the lemon, then the dry ingredients, which have previously been combined by stirring together in a pan with a fork without sifting. It's better to sift, but I do everything the fast way.

Finally, fold in the egg whites and pour the batter in two bread loaf pans with the bottoms lined with wax paper. Bake at 350° for about ½ hour; lower to 325° and bake 30 to 45 minutes longer.

After cooling this cake and sampling it, we decided on several variations, including serving a slice topped with ice cream or whipped cream and garnished with strawberries, raspberries, or other fruit. However, we restrained ourselves.

George got lucky because I recently turned out an orange pound cake that is so delicious and easy to make, he decided to bake one himself, and *did*. Try it.

ORANGE POUND CAKE

2 cups unbleached flour
1 cup sugar
1½ teaspoons baking powder
¾ teaspoon salt

½ cup corn oil margarine
1 tablespoon grated orange rind
¾ cup orange juice
2 eggs

In the large mixer bowl, combine the flour, sugar, baking powder, salt, margarine, orange rind, and orange juice. Beat 2 minutes at medium speed. Add the eggs and beat 2 minutes more. Bake in a loaf pan, lined with wax paper, for 1 hour at 350°.

Here are other cake favorites of ours.

MINCEMEAT CAKE

1 pint prepared mincemeat	1 teaspoon baking powder
¾ cup honey or sugar	1 teaspoon baking soda
½ cup corn oil	½ teaspoon salt
2¼ cups flour	½ cup nuts (optional)

Combine the mincemeat, honey or sugar, and oil. Stir the mixture into the dry ingredients, which have been combined in a mixing bowl. Add the nuts and pour the batter into a 9 x 13 inch pan, lined with wax paper. Bake at 350° about 50 minutes.

I substitute ¼ cup wheat germ for the same amount of flour and add 1 tablespoon soya powder to the dry ingredients. I also add 2 eggs, combining the yolks with the mincemeat, honey, and oil and folding in the stiffly beaten egg whites last. I use my homemade green tomato mincemeat, too. Because of George's hangup about nuts, I just strew chopped nuts on top of the cake batter before baking. When serving squares of the cake, embellish them with a dollop of plain yogurt, sour cream, or applesauce.

AULD LANG SYNE CAKE

2 eggs	1½ teaspoons baking powder
1 cup sugar	½ teaspoon baking soda
½ cup corn oil	1 teaspoon cinnamon
½ cup milk	½ teaspoon nutmeg
2 cups flour	1 cup raisins
¼ cup wheat germ	1 cup candied fruit
¼ cup powdered milk (optional)	½ cup nuts (optional)

Beat the eggs until light. Add the sugar, oil, and milk. Combine the dry ingredients, and add. Stir in the raisins and candied fruit. Pour the batter in a 9 x 13 inch pan, lined with wax paper, and bake at 350° about 50 minutes. Honey may be substituted for part of the sugar.

Here is a fun pastry that always went over big at my children's parties. The batter is easy and inexpensive, but a patty shell set or rosette iron is necessary. I have my mother's, which has an L-shaped handle and interchangeable heads.

ROSETTES

2 eggs	¾ cup milk
¼ teaspoon salt	1 cup flour
1 tablespoon sugar or honey	½ teaspoon vanilla
1 tablespoon corn oil	

Beat all the ingredients together for a thin smooth batter.

Heat 2 or 3 inches of oil in a skillet to frying temperature. Heat the iron mold in the oil a few seconds. Then dip it into the batter, being careful not to let any run over the top of the mold. Return the batter-covered mold to the hot oil, immersing it for a few seconds. Work the rosette off the mold with a fork and cook it for about 15 seconds on each side. Often the rosette will fall off without prying with a fork. Drain on paper towel and dust with confectioners' sugar, when cool.

One of the most elegant of company desserts is one of the easiest to make. Eclair or cream puff shells can be made in quantity and frozen for future use. This is my healthier version.

ECLAIRS OR CREAM PUFFS

1 cup water	1 cup stone-ground whole wheat
½ cup corn oil	flour
¼ teaspoon salt	4 eggs

Combine the water, oil, and salt and bring to a boil. Add the flour all at once and stir the mixture quickly over the stove cooking unit until a mass forms and leaves the sides of the pan. Cool slightly, then add eggs one at a time, beating after each until well blended. After adding the final egg, beat about 3 minutes until the mass is smooth and satiny. Form cream puffs by placing teaspoonfuls of dough about 2 inches apart on baking pans. To make eclairs, shape the dough about 1 inch wide, 4 inches long, and about ½ inch thick. I usually make eclairs and use my ovenliner pans, which do not need oiling.

Bake for 10 minutes at 425°, then lower oven to 350° for about 25 minutes, or until the shells are dry. Shut off the oven and leave the shells inside for complete drying. (You can peek once in a while for reassurance.)

To serve, split the shells, fill with vanilla ice cream, and frost with

Judy's chocolate cake icing. To make entertaining easier, I prepare the eclairs and freeze them on trays the day before, taking them out of the freezer just before serving dinner—they thaw by dessert time. Shells may also be bagged in plastic and frozen for preparation at a future time.

For those who prefer cream filling, here is an easy one made from scratch, preferable to the packaged puddings.

VANILLA CREAM FILLING

⅔ cup sugar	2 cups milk
6 tablespoons flour	2 beaten eggs
pinch of salt	2 teaspoons vanilla

Combine the sugar, flour, and salt in a bowl. Add a little of the milk to form a thin paste. Scald the remaining milk and gradually add the paste, stirring constantly until the milk mixture thickens. Pour some of the hot milk mixture over the beaten eggs gradually; then return the egg mixture to the milk mixture and bring to a boil, stirring constantly. Cool and add vanilla.

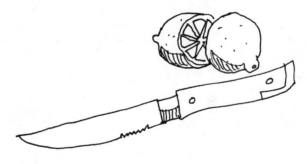

Index